LAOTZU'S TAO AND WU WEI

TRANSLATION BY
DWIGHT GODDARD

WU WEI

AN INTERPRETATION BY
HENRI BOREL

TRANSLATED BY
M. E. REYNOLDS

NEW YORK
BRENTANO'S
PUBLISHERS

INTRODUCTION

I LOVE LAOTZU! That is the reason I offer another interpretative translation, and try to print and bind it attractively. I want you to appreciate this wise and kindly old man, and come to love him. He was perhaps the first of scholars (6th century B.C.) to have a vision of spiritual reality, and he tried so hard to explain it to others, only, in the end, to wander away into the Great Unknown in pathetic discouragement. Everything was against him; his friends misunderstood him; others made fun of him.

Even the written characters which he must use to preserve his thought conspired against him. They were only five thousand in all, and were ill adapted to express mystical and abstract ideas. When these characters are translated accurately, the translation is necessarily awkward and obscure. Sinologues have unintentionally done him an injustice by their very scholarship. I have tried to peer through the clumsy characters into his heart and prayed that love for him would make me wise to understand aright.

I hate scholarship that would deny his existence, or arrogant erudition that says patronizingly, "Oh, yes, there doubtless was some one who wrote some of the characteristic sonnets,

1

but most of them are an accumulation through the centuries of verses that have similar structure, and all have been changed and amended until it is better to call the book a collection of aphorisms."

Shame on scholarship when, sharing the visions of the illuminati, they deride them!

There are three great facts in China to-day that vouch for Laotzu. First, the presence of Taoism, which was suggested by his teachings, not founded upon them. This is explained by the inability of the scholars, who immediately followed him, to understand and appreciate the spirituality of his teachings. Second, Confucian dislike for Laotzian ideas, which is explained by their opposition to Confucian ethics. Third, and the greatest fact of all, is the characteristic traits of Chinese nature, namely, passivity, submissiveness and moral concern, all of which find an adequate cause and source in the teachings of Laotzu.

An interesting fact in regard to the thought of Laotzu is this. Although for two thousand years he has been misunderstood and derided, to-day the very best of scientific and philosophic thought, which gathers about what is known as Vitalism, is in full accord with Laotzu's idea of the Tao. Every reference that is made to-day to a Cosmic Urge, Vital Impulse, and Creative Principle can be said of the Tao. Everything that can be said of Plato's Ideas and Forms and of Cosmic Love as being the creative expression of God can be said of the Tao. When Christian scholars came to translate the Logos of St. John, they were satisfied to use the word "Tao."

It is true that Laotzu's conception of the Tao was limited to a conception of a universal, creative principle. He apparently had no conception of personality, which the Christians ascribe to God, in connection with it, but he ascribed so much of wisdom and benevolence to it that his conception fell little short of personality. To Laotzu, the Tao is the universal and eternal principle which forms and conditions everything; it is that intangible cosmic influence which harmonizes all things and brings them to fruition; it is the norm and standard of truth and morality. Laotzu did more than entertain an intelligent opinion of Tao as a creative principle; he had a devout and religious sentiment towards it: "He loved the Tao as a son cherishes and reveres his mother."

There are three key words in the thought of Laotzu: Tao, Teh, and Wu Wei. They are all difficult to translate. The simple meaning of Tao is "way," but it also has a wide variety of other meanings. Dr. Paul Carus translates it, "Reason," but apologizes for so doing. If forced to offer a translation we would suggest Creative Principle, but much prefer to leave it untranslated.

The character, "Teh," is usually translated "virtue." This is correct as a mere translation of the character, but is in no sense adequate to the content of the thought in Laotzu's mind. To him, Teh meant precisely what is meant in the account of the healing of the woman who touched the hem of Jesus' robe: "Jesus was conscious that *virtue* had passed from him." Teh includes the meaning of vitality, of virility, of beauty and the harmony that we think of as that part of life that is abounding and joyous. The third word is the negative expression, "Wu Wei." Translated, this means "not acting," or "non-assertion." When Laotzu urges men to "wu wei," he is not urging them to laziness or asceticism. He means that all men are to cherish that wise humility and diffidence and selflessness which comes from a consciousness that the Tao is infinitely wise and good, and that the part of human wisdom is to hold one's self in such a restrained and receptive manner that the Tao may find one a suitable and conforming channel for its purpose. The title of Laotzu's book, Tao Teh King, is carelessly translated, The Way of Virtue Classic, or The Way and Virtue Classic. This is very inadequate. The Vitality of the Tao is very much better.

Most commentators think that Laotzu's teachings fit in especially well with Buddhist philosophy This conclusion is arrived at by the common interpretation of wu wei as submission that will logically end in absorption of the spirit in Tao as Nirvana. This understanding of wu wei, which Henri Borel shares in a measure, is, we believe, incorrect, inasmuch as Laotzu consistently teaches a *finding* of life rather than a losing of it. Laotzu's conception of Tao as the underived Source of all things, finding expression through spiritual Teh in universal creative activity, is very close to Plato's doctrine of the good as the One ineffable Source of all things, whose Ideas and Forms of Goodness, Truth and Beauty radiated outward as spiritual logoi in creative activity through Spirit, Soul and Nature to the farthest confines of matter.

While it is true that Laotzu's teachings would find little in common with the Old Testament anthropomorphic autocracy, and would find almost nothing in common with the modern Ritschlean system of ethical idealism which has for its basis a naturalistic evolution of human society by means of philanthropy, laws, cultural civilizations, and human governments backed by force of arms, nevertheless his teachings are entirely in harmony with that Christian philosophy of the Logos, which is a heritage from the Greeks, through Plato, Philo, St. Paul, Plotinus, and Augustine, and which is the basis of the mystical faith of the Christian saints of all ages. While Laotzu would find little in common with the busy, impertinent activities of so-called Christian statesman building by statecraft and war, he would find much in common with Apostolic Christianity which held itself aloof from current politics and refused to enter the army, content to live simply, quietly, full of faith and humble benevolence.

And most of all would he find himself in sympathy with the teacher of Nazareth. At almost every Sonnet, one thinks of some corresponding expression of Jesus, who had a very similar conception of God, but who recognized in Him that personal element of Love which made God not only Creative Principle but Heavenly Father.

Laotzu's vision of the virile harmony, goodness, and Spirituality of the Tao was what Jesus saw as the Fatherhood of God, self-expressing his love-nature endlessly in all creative effort, and, through universal intuition, endlessly drawing his creation back to himself in grateful and humble affection. Laotzu saw in a glass darkly what Jesus saw face to face in all his glory, the Divine Tao, God as creative and redemptive Love.

As you read these verses, forget the words and phrases, poor material and poor workmanship at best, look through them for the soul of Laotzu. It is there revealed, but so imperfectly that it is only an apparition of a soul. But if by it, vague as it is, you come to love Laotzu, you will catch beyond him fleeting glimpses of the splendid visions that so possessed his soul, visions of Infinite Goodness, Humility and Beauty radiating from the Heart of creation.

DWIGHT GODDARD.

ALL WE KNOW ABOUT LAOTZU

SZE MA–CH'IEN (136–85 B.C.) wrote that Laotzu was born of the Li family of Ch'u-jen Village, Li County, K'u Province, Ch'u State. His proper name was Err, his official name was Poh-yang, his posthumous title was Yueh-tan. He held the position of custodian of the secret archives of the State of Cheu.

Confucius went to Cheu to consult Laotzu about certain ceremonials; Laotzu told him: "The bones of these sages, concerning whom you inquire, have long since decayed, only their teachings remain. If a superior man is understood by his age, he rises to honor, but not being understood, his name is like a vagrant seed blown about by the wind. I have heard it said that a good merchant conceals his treasures, as though his warehouses were empty. The sage of highest worth assumes a countenance and outward mien as though he were stupid. Put aside your haughty airs, your many needs, affected robes and exaggerated importance. These add no real value to your person. That is my advice to you, and it is all I have to offer."

Confucius departed and when he later described to his students his visit to Laotzu, he said: "I understand about the habits of birds, how

7

they can fly; how fish can swim; and animals run. For the running we can make snares, for the swimming we can make nets, for the flying we can make arrows. But for the dragon, I cannot know how he ascends on the winds and clouds to heaven. I have just seen Laotzu. Can it be said, he is as difficult to understand as the dragon? He teaches the vitality of Tao. His doctrine appears to lead one to aspire after self-effacement and obscurity."

Laotzu lived in Cheu for a long time; he prophesied the decay of that state and in consequence was obliged to depart, and went to the frontier. The officer at the border post was Yin-hi, who said to Laotzu, "If you are going to leave us, will you not write a book by which we may remember you?" Thereupon Laotzu wrote a book of sonnets in two parts, comprising in all about five thousand characters. In this book he discussed his conception of the Vitality of the Tao. He left this book with the soldier, and departed, no one knows whither.

TAO TEH KING

I

WHAT IS THE TAO

The Tao that can be understood cannot be the primal, or cosmic, Tao, just as an idea that can be expressed in words cannot be the infinite idea.

And yet this ineffable Tao was the source of all spirit and matter, and being expressed was the mother of all created things.

Therefore not to desire the things of sense is to know the freedom of spirituality; and to desire is to learn the limitation of matter. These two things spirit and matter, so different in nature, have the same origin. This unity of origin is the mystery of mysteries, but it is the gateway to spirituality.

II

SELF-DEVELOPMENT

When every one recognizes beauty to be only a masquerade, then it is simply ugliness. In the same way goodness, if it is not sincere, is not goodness. So existence and non-existence are incompatible. The difficult and easy are mutually opposites. Just as the long and the short,

11

the high and the low, the loud and soft, the
before and the behind, are all opposites and
each reveals the other.

Therefore the wise man is not conspicuous in
his affairs or given to much talking. Though
troubles arise he is not irritated. He produces
but does not own; he acts but claims no merit;
he builds but does not dwell therein; and because
he does not dwell therein he never departs.

III

QUIETING PEOPLE

Neglecting to praise the worthy deters people
from emulating them; just as not prizing rare
treasures deters a man from becoming a thief;
or ignoring the things which awaken desire keeps
the heart at rest.

Therefore the wise ruler does not suggest
unnecessary things, but seeks to satisfy the minds
of his people. He seeks to allay appetites but
strengthen bones. He ever tries by keeping
people in ignorance to keep them satisfied and
those who have knowledge he restrains from
evil. If he, himself, practices restraint then everything is in quietness.

IV

TAO, WITHOUT ORIGIN

The Tao appears to be emptiness but it is never
exhausted. Oh, it is profound! It appears to
have preceded everything. It dulls its own

sharpness, unravels its own fetters, softens its own brightness, identifies itself with its own dust.

Oh, it is tranquil! It appears infinite; I do not know from what it proceeds. It even appears to be antecedent to the Lord.

V

IMPARTIALITY

Heaven and earth are not like humans, they are impartial. They regard all things as insignificant, as though they were playthings made of straw. The wise man is also impartial. To him all men are alike and unimportant. The space between heaven and earth is like a bellows, it is empty but does not collapse; it moves and more and more issues. A gossip is soon empty, it is doubtful if he can be impartial.

VI

THE INFINITUDE OF CREATIVE EFFORT

The Spirit of the perennial spring is said to be immortal, she is called the Mysterious One. The Mysterious One is typical of the source of heaven and earth. It is continually and endlessly issuing and without effort.

VII

HUMILITY

Heaven is eternal, earth is lasting. The reason why heaven and earth are eternal and lasting is

because they do not live for themselves; that
is the reason they will ever endure.

Therefore the wise man will keep his personality out of sight and because of so doing he
will become notable. He subordinates his personality and therefore it is preserved.

Is it not because he is disinterested, that his
own interests are conserved?

VIII

THE NATURE OF GOODNESS

True goodness is like water, in that it benefits
everything and harms nothing. Like water it
ever seeks the lowest place, the place that all
others avoid. It is closely kin to the Tao.

For a dwelling it chooses the quiet meadow;
for a heart the circling eddy. In generosity it
is kind; in speech it is sincere; in authority it
is order; in affairs it is ability; in movement it is
rhythm.

Inasmuch as it is always peaceable it is never
rebuked.

IX

MODERATION

Continuing to fill a pail after it is full the water
will be wasted. Continuing to grind an axe
after it is sharp will soon wear it away.

Who can protect a public hall crowded with
gold and jewels? The pride of wealth and position brings about their own misfortune. To win

true merit, to preserve just fame, the personality must be retiring. This is the heavenly Tao.

X

WHAT IS POSSIBLE

By patience the animal spirits can be disciplined. By self-control one can unify the character. By close attention to the will, compelling gentleness, one can become like a little child. By purifying the subconscious desires one may be without fault. In ruling his country, if the wise magistrate loves his people, he can avoid compulsion.

In measuring out rewards, the wise magistrate will act like a mother bird. While sharply penetrating into every corner, he may appear to be unsuspecting. While quickening and feeding his people, he will be producing but without pride of ownership. He will benefit but without claim of reward. He will persuade, but not compel by force. This is teh, the profoundest virtue.

XI

THE VALUE OF NON-EXISTENCE

Although the wheel has thirty spokes its utility lies in the emptiness of the hub. The jar is made by kneading clay, but its usefulness consists in its capacity. A room is made by cutting out windows and doors through the walls, but the space the walls contain measures the room's value.

In the same way matter is necessary to form, but the value of reality lies in its immateriality.

(Or thus: a material body is necessary to existence, but the value of a life is measured by its immaterial soul.)

XII

AVOIDING DESIRE

An excess of light blinds the human eye; an excess of noise ruins the ear; an excess of condiments deadens the taste. The effect of too much horse racing and hunting is bad, and the lure of hidden treasure tempts one to do evil.

Therefore the wise man attends to the inner significance of things and does not concern himself with outward appearances. Therefore he ignores matter and seeks the spirit.

XIII

LOATHING SHAME

Favor and disgrace are alike to be feared, just as too great care or anxiety are bad for the body.

Why are favor and disgrace alike to be feared? To be favored is humiliating; to obtain it is as much to be dreaded as to lose it. To lose favor is to be in disgrace and of course is to be dreaded.

Why are excessive care and great anxiety alike bad for one? The very reason I have anxiety is because I have a body. If I have not body why would I be anxious?

Therefore if he who administers the empire,

esteems it as his own body, then he is worthy to be trusted with the empire.

XIV

IN PRAISE OF THE PROFOUND

It is unseen because it is colorless; it is unheard because it is soundless; when seeking to grasp it, it eludes one, because it is incorporeal.

Because of these qualities it cannot be examined, and yet they form an essential unity. Superficially it appears abstruse, but in its depths it is not obscure. It has been nameless forever! It appears and then disappears. It is what is known as the form of the formless, the image of the imageless. It is called the transcendental, its face (or destiny) cannot be seen in front, or its back (or origin) behind.

But by holding fast to the Tao of the ancients, the wise man may understand the present, because he knows the origin of the past. This is the clue to the Tao.

XV

THAT WHICH REVEALS TEH

In olden times the ones who were considered worthy to be called masters were subtle, spiritual, profound, wise. Their thoughts could not be easily understood.

Since they were hard to understand I will try to make them clear. They were cautious like men wading a river in winter. They were reluctant like men who feared their neighbors.

They were reserved like guests in the presence of
their host. They were elusive like ice at the
point of melting. They were like unseasoned
wood. They were like a valley between high
mountains. They were obscure like troubled
waters. (They were cautious because they were
conscious of the deeper meanings of life and its
possibilities.)

We can clarify troubled waters by slowly quiet-
ing them. We can bring the unconscious to life
by slowly moving them. But he who has the
secret of the Tao does not desire for more. Being
content, he is able to mature without desire to
be newly fashioned.

XVI
RETURNING TO THE SOURCE

Seek to attain an open mind (the summit of
vacuity). Seek composure (the essence of tranquillity).

All things are in process, rising and returning.
Plants come to blossom, but only to return to
the root. Returning to the root is like seeking
tranquillity; it is moving towards its destiny.
To move toward destiny is like eternity. To
know eternity is enlightenment, and not to recognize eternity brings disorder and evil.

Knowing eternity makes one comprehensive;
comprehension makes one broadminded; breadth
of vision brings nobility; nobility is like heaven.

The heavenly is like Tao. Tao is the Eternal.
The decay of the body is not to be feared.

XVII
SIMPLICITY OF HABIT

When great men rule, subjects know little of their existence. Rulers who are less great win the affection and praise of their subjects. A common ruler is feared by his subjects, and an unworthy ruler is despised.

When a ruler lacks faith, you may seek in vain for it among his subjects.

How carefully a wise ruler chooses his words. He performs deeds, and accumulates merit! Under such a ruler the people think they are ruling themselves.

XVIII
THE PALLIATION OF THE INFERIOR

When the great Tao is lost sight of, we still have the *idea* of benevolence and righteousness. Prudence and wisdom come to mind when we see great hypocrisy. When relatives are unfriendly, we still have the *teachings* of filial piety and paternal affection. When the state and the clan are in confusion and disorder, we still have the *ideals* of loyalty and faithfulness.

XIX
RETURN TO SIMPLICITY

Abandon the show of saintliness and relinquish excessive prudence, then people will benefit a hundredfold. Abandon ostentatious benevolence and conspicuous righteousness, then people will re-

turn to the primal virtues of filial piety and paren-
tal affection.   Abandon cleverness and relinquish
gains, then thieves and robbers will disappear.

Here are three fundamentals on which to de-
pend, wherein culture is insufficient.   Therefore
let all men hold to that which is reliable, namely,
recognize simplicity, cherish purity, reduce one's
possessions, diminish one's desires.

XX

THE OPPOSITE OF THE COMMONPLACE

Avoid learning if you would have no anxiety.
The "yes" and the "yea" differ very little, but
the contrast between good and evil is very great.
That which is not feared by the people is not
worth fearing.   But, oh, the difference, the
desolation, the vastness, between ignorance and
the limitless expression of the Tao.

*(The balance of this sonnet is devoted to show-
ing the difference between the careless state of
the common people and his own vision of the
Tao.   It is one of the most pathetic expressions
of human loneliness, from lack of appreciation,
ever written.   It is omitted here that it might
serve for the closing sonnet and valedictory.)*

XXI

THE HEART OF EMPTINESS

All the innumerable forms of teh correspond
to the norm of Tao, but the nature of the Tao's
activity is infinitely abstract and illusive.   Illusive and obscure, indeed, but at its heart are

forms and types. Vague and illusive, indeed, but at its heart is all being. Unfathomable and obscure, indeed, but at its heart is all spirit, and spirit is reality. At its heart is truth.

From of old its expression is unceasing, it has been present at all beginnings. How do I know that its nature is thus? By this same Tao.

XXII

INCREASE BY HUMILITY

At that time the deficient will be made perfect; the distorted will be straightened; the empty will be filled; the worn out will be renewed; those having little will obtain and those having much will be overcome.

Therefore the wise man, embracing unity as he does, will become the world's model. Not pushing himself forward he will become enlightened; not asserting himself he will become distinguished; not boasting of himself he will acquire merit; not approving himself he will endure. Forasmuch as he will not quarrel, the world will not quarrel with him.

Is the old saying, "The crooked shall be made straight," a false saying? Indeed, no! They will be perfected and return rejoicing.

XXIII

EMPTINESS AND NOT-DOING (WU WEI)

Taciturnity is natural to man. A whirlwind never outlasts the morning, nor a violent rain the day. What is the cause? It is heaven and earth. If even heaven and earth are not constant, much less can man be.

Therefore he who pursues his affairs in the spirit of Tao will become Tao-like. He who pursues his affairs with teh, will become teh-like. He who pursues his affairs with loss, identifies himself with loss.

He who identifies himself with Tao, Tao rejoices to guide. He who identifies himself with teh, teh rejoices to reward. And he who identifies himself with loss, loss rejoices to ruin.

If his faith fail, he will receive no reward of faith.

XXIV

TROUBLES AND MERIT

It is not natural to stand on tiptoe, or being astride one does not walk. One who displays himself is not bright, or one who asserts himself cannot shine. A self-approving man has no merit, nor does one who praises himself grow.

The relation of these things (self-display, self-assertion, self-approval) to Tao is the same as offal is to food. They are excrescences from the system; they are detestable; Tao does not dwell in them.

XXV

DESCRIBING THE MYSTERIOUS

There is Being that is all-inclusive and that existed before Heaven and Earth. Calm, indeed, and incorporeal! It is alone and changeless!

Everywhere it functions unhindered. It thereby becomes the world's mother. I do not know its nature; if I try to characterize it, I will call it Tao.

If forced to give it a name, I will call it the Great. The Great is evasive, the evasive is the distant, the distant is ever coming near. Tao is Great. So is Heaven great, and so is Earth and so also is the representative of Heaven and Earth.

Man is derived from nature, nature is derived from Heaven, Heaven is derived from Tao. Tao is self-derived.

XXVI

THE VIRTUE (TEH) OF DIGNITY

The heavy is the root of the light; the quiet is master of motion. Therefore the wise man in all the experience of the day will not depart from dignity. Though he be surrounded with sights that are magnificent, he will remain calm and unconcerned.

How does it come to pass that the Emperor, master of ten thousand chariots, has lost the mastery of the Empire? Because being flippant himself, he has lost the respect of his subjects; being passionate himself, he has lost the control of the Empire.

XXVII

THE FUNCTION OF SKILL

Good walkers leave no tracks, good speakers make no errors, good counters need no abacus,

good wardens have no need for bolts and locks
for no one can get by them. Good binders can
dispense with rope and cord, yet none can unloose
their hold.

Therefore the wise man trusting in goodness
always saves men, for there is no outcast to him.
Trusting in goodness he saves all things for there
is nothing valueless to him. This is recognizing
concealed values.

Therefore the good man is the instructor of
the evil man, and the evil man is the good man's
wealth. He who does not esteem his instructors
or value his wealth, though he be otherwise intelligent, becomes confused. Herein lies the
significance of spirituality.

XXVIII

RETURNING TO SIMPLICITY

He who knows his manhood and understands
his womanhood becomes useful like the valleys
of earth (which bring water). Being like the
valleys of earth, eternal vitality (teh) will not
depart from him, he will come again to the nature
of a little child.

He who knows his innocence and recognizes
his sin becomes the world's model. Being a
world's model, infinite teh will not fail, he will
return to the Absolute.

He who knows the glory of his nature and
recognizes also his limitations becomes useful
like the world's valleys. Being like the world's

valleys, eternal teh will not fail him, he will revert to simplicity.

Radiating simplicity he will make of men vessels of usefulness. The wise man then will employ them as officials and chiefs. A great administration of such will harm no one.

XXIX

NOT FORCING THINGS (WU WEI)

One who desires to take and remake the Empire will fail. The Empire is a divine thing that cannot be remade. He who attempts it will only mar it.

He who seeks to grasp it, will lose it. People differ, some lead, others follow; some are ardent, others are formal; some are strong, others weak; some succeed, others fail. Therefore the wise man practices moderation; he abandons pleasure, extravagance and indulgence.

XXX

BE STINGY OF WAR

When the magistrate follows Tao, he has no need to resort to force of arms to strengthen the Empire, because his business methods alone will show good returns.

Briars and thorns grow rank where an army camps. Bad harvests are the sequence of a great war. The good ruler will be resolute and then stop, he dare not take by force. One should be resolute but not boastful; resolute but not haughty; resolute but not arrogant; resolute but yielding when it cannot be avoided; resolute but he must not resort to violence.

By a resort to force, things flourish for a time but then decay. This is not like the Tao and that which is not Tao-like will soon cease.

XXXI

AVOIDING WAR

Even successful arms, among all implements, are unblessed. All men come to detest them. Therefore the one who follows Tao does not rely on them. Arms are of all tools unblessed, they are not the implements of a wise man. Only as a last resort does he use them.

Peace and quietude are esteemed by the wise man, and even when victorious he does not rejoice, because rejoicing over a victory is the same as rejoicing over the killing of men. If he rejoices over killing men, do you think he will ever really master the Empire?

In propitious affairs the place of honor is the left, but in unpropitious affairs we honor the right.

The strong man while at home esteems the left as the place of honor, but when armed for war it is as though he esteems the right hand, the place of less honor.

Thus a funeral ceremony is so arranged. The place of a subordinate army officer is also on the left and the place of his superior officer is on the right. The killing of men fills multitudes

with sorrow; we lament with tears because of it,
and rightly honor the victor as if he was attend-
ing a funeral ceremony.

XXXII
THE VIRTUE (TEH) OF HOLINESS

Tao in its eternal aspect is unnamable. Its
simplicity appears insignificant, but the whole
world cannot control it. If princes and kings
employ it every one of themselves will pay willing
homage. Heaven and Earth by it are harmoni-
ously combined and drop sweet dew. People
will have no need of rulers, because of themselves
they will be righteous.

As soon as Tao expresses itself in `orderly
creation then it becomes comprehensible. When
one recognizes the presence of Tao he understands
where to stop. Knowing where to stop he is free
from danger.

To illustrate the nature of Tao's place in the
universe: Tao is like the brooks and streams in
their relation to the great rivers and the ocean.

XXXIII
THE VIRTUE (TEH) OF DISCRIMINATION

He who knows others is intelligent; he who
understands himself is enlightened; he who is
able to conquer others has force, but he who is
able to control himself is mighty. He who ap-
preciates contentment is wealthy.

He who dares to act has nerve; if he can main-

tain his position he will endure, but he, who
dying does not perish, is immortal.

XXXIV

THE PERFECTION OF TRUST

Great Tao is all pervading! It can be on both
the right hand and the left. Everything relies
upon it for their existence, and it does not fail
them. It acquires merit but covets not the
title. It lovingly nourishes everything, but does
not claim the rights of ownership. It has no
desires, it can be classed with the small. Everything returns to it, yet it does not claim the
right of ownership. It can be classed with the
great.

Therefore the wise man to the end will not pose
as a great man, and by so doing will express his
true greatness.

XXXV

THE VIRTUE (TEH) OF BENEVOLENCE

The world will go to him who grasps this Great
Principle; they will seek and not be injured;
they will find contentment, peace and rest.

Music and dainties attract the passing people,
while Tao's reality seems insipid. Indeed it has
no taste, when looked at there is not enough
seen to be prized, when listened for, it can
scarcely be heard, but the use of it is inexhaustible.

XXXVI

EXPLANATION OF A PARADOX

That which has a tendency to contract must first have been extended; that which has a tendency to weaken itself must first have been strong; that which shows a tendency to destroy itself must first have been raised up; that which shows a tendency to scatter must first have been gathered.

This is the explanation of a seeming contradiction: the tender and yielding conquer the rigid and strong (*i.e.*, spirit is stronger than matter, persuasion than force). The fish would be foolish to seek escape from its natural environment. There is no gain to a nation to compel by a show of force.

XXXVII

ADMINISTERING THE GOVERNMENT

Tao is apparently inactive (wu wei) and yet nothing remains undone. If princes and kings desire to keep everything in order, they must first reform themselves. (If princes and kings would follow the example of Tao, then all things will reform themselves.) If they still desire to change, I would pacify them by the simplicity of the ineffable Tao.

This simplicity will end desire, and if desire be absent there is quietness. All people will of themselves be satisfied.

XXXVIII

A DISCUSSION ABOUT TEH

Essential teh makes no show of virtue, and therefore it is really virtuous. Inferior virtue never loses sight of itself and therefore it is no longer virtue. Essential virtue is characterized by lack of self-assertion (wu wei) and therefore is unpretentious. Inferior virtue is acting a part and thereby is only pretense.

Superior benevolence in a way is acting but does not thereby become pretentious. Excessive righteousness is acting and does thereby become pretentious. Excessive propriety is acting, but where no one responds to it, it stretches its arm and enforces obedience.

Therefore when one loses Tao there is still teh; one may lose teh and benevolence remains; one may forsake benevolence and still hold to righteousness; one may lose righteousness and propriety remains.

Propriety, alone, reduces loyalty and good faith to a shadow, and it is the beginning of disorder. Tradition is the mere flower of the Tao and had its origin in ignorance.

Therefore the great man of affairs conforms to the spirit and not to external appearance. He goes on to fruitage and does not rest in the show of blossom. He avoids mere propriety and practices true benevolence.

XXXIX

THE ROOT OF AUTHORITY

It has been said of old, only those who attain unity attain self-hood. . . . Heaven attained unity and thereby is space. Earth attained unity, thereby it is solid. Spirit attained unity, thereby it became mind. Valleys attained unity, therefore rivers flow down them. All things have unity and thereby have life. Princes and kings as they attain unity become standards of conduct for the nation. And the highest unity is that which produces unity.

If heaven were not space it might crack, if earth were not solid it might bend. If spirits were not unified into mind they might vanish, if valleys were not adapted to rivers they would be parched. Everything if it were not for life would burn up. Even princes and kings if they overestimate themselves and cease to be standards will presumably fall.

Therefore nobles find their roots among the commoners; the high is always founded upon the low. The reason why princes and kings speak of themselves as orphans, inferiors and unworthy, is because they recognize that their roots run down to the common life; is it not so?

If a carriage goes to pieces it is no longer a carriage, its unity is gone. A true self-hood does not desire to be overvalued as a gem, nor to be undervalued as a mere stone.

XL

AVOIDING ACTIVITY

Retirement is characteristic of Tao just as weakness appears to be a characteristic of its activity.

Heaven and earth and everything are produced from existence, but existence comes from non-existence. . . .

XLI

THE UNREALITY OF APPEARANCE

The superior scholar when he considers Tao earnestly practices it; an average scholar listening to Tao sometimes follows it and sometimes loses it; an inferior scholar listening to Tao ridicules it. Were it not thus ridiculed it could not be regarded as Tao.

Therefore the writer says: Those who are most illumined by Tao are the most obscure. Those advanced in Tao are most retiring. Those best guided by Tao are the least prepossessing.

The high in virtue (teh) resemble a lowly valley; the whitest are most likely to be put to shame; the broadest in virtue resemble the inefficient. The most firmly established in virtue resemble the remiss. The simplest chastity resembles the fickle, the greatest square has no corner, the largest vessel is never filled. The greatest sound is void of speech, the greatest form has no shape. Tao is obscure and without name, and yet it is precisely this Tao that alone can give and complete.

XLII

THE TRANSFORMATION OF TAO

Tao produces unity; unity produces duality; duality produces trinity; trinity produces all things. All things bear the negative principle (yin) and embrace the positive principle (yang). Immaterial vitality, the third principle (chi), makes them harmonious.

Those things which are detested by the common people, namely to be called orphans, inferiors, and unworthies, are the very things kings and lords take for titles. There are some things which it is a gain to lose, and a loss to gain.

I am teaching the same things which are taught by others. But the strong and aggressive ones do not obtain a natural death (*i.e.*, self-confident teachers do not succeed). I alone expound the basis of the doctrine of the Tao.

XLIII

THE FUNCTION OF THE UNIVERSAL

The most tender things of creation race over the hardest.

A non-material existence enters into the most impenetrable.

I therefore recognize an advantage in the doctrine of not doing (wu wei) and not speaking.

But there are few in the world who obtain the advantage of non-assertion (wu wei) and silence.

XLIV

PRECEPTS

Which is nearer, a name or a person? Which is more, personality or treasure? Is it more painful to gain or to suffer loss?

Extreme indulgence certainly greatly wastes. Much hoarding certainly invites severe loss.

A contented person is not despised. One who knows when to stop is not endangered; he will be able therefore to continue.

XLV

THE VIRTUE (TEH) OF GREATNESS

Extreme perfection seems imperfect, its function is not exhausted. Extreme fullness appears empty, its function is not exercised.

Extreme straightness appears crooked; great skill, clumsy; great eloquence, stammering. Motion conquers cold, quietude conquers heat. Not greatness but purity and clearness are the world's standard.

XLVI

LIMITATION OF DESIRE

When the world yields to Tao, race horses will be used to haul manure. When the world ignores Tao war horses are pastured on the public common.

There is no sin greater than desire. There is no misfortune greater than discontent. There is no calamity greater than acquisitiveness.

Therefore to know extreme contentment is simply to be content.

XLVII
SEEING THE DISTANT

Not going out of the door I have knowledge of the world. Not peeping through the window I perceive heaven's Tao. The more one wanders to a distance the less he knows.

Therefore the wise man does not wander about but he understands, he does not see things but he defines them, he does not labor yet he completes.

XLVIII
TO FORGET KNOWLEDGE

He who attends daily to learning increases in learning. He who practices Tao daily diminishes. Again and again he humbles himself. Thus he attains to non-doing (wu wei). He practices non-doing and yet there is nothing left undone.

To command the empire one must not employ craft. If one uses craft he is not fit to command the empire.

XLIX
THE VIRTUE (TEH) OF TRUST

The wise man has no fixed heart; in the hearts of the people he finds his own. The good he treats with goodness; the not-good he also treats with goodness, for teh is goodness. The faithful ones he treats with good faith; the unfaithful he also treats with good faith, for teh is good faith.

The wise man lives in the world but he lives cautiously, dealing with the world cautiously. He universalizes his heart; the people give him their eyes and ears, but he treats them as his children.

L

ESTEEM LIFE

Life is a going forth; death is a returning home. Of ten, three are seeking life, three are seeking death, and three are dying. What is the reason? Because they live in life's experience. (Only one is immortal.)

I hear it said that the sage when he travels is never attacked by rhinoceros or tiger, and when coming among soldiers does not fear their weapons. The rhinoceros would find no place to horn him, nor the tiger a place for his claws, nor could soldiers wound him. What is the reason? Because he is invulnerable.

LI

TEH AS A NURSE

Tao gives life to all creatures; teh feeds them; materiality shapes them; energy completes them.

Therefore among all things there is none that does not honor Tao and esteem teh. Honor for Tao and esteem for teh is never compelled, it is always spontaneous. Therefore Tao gives life to them, but teh nurses them, raises them, nurtures, completes, matures, rears, protects them.

Tao gives life to them but makes no claim of ownership; teh forms them but makes no claim upon them, raises them but does not rule them. This is profound vitality (teh).

LII

RETURN TO ORIGIN

When creation began, Tao became the world's mother. When one knows one's mother he will in turn know that he is her son. When he recognizes his sonship, he will in turn keep to his mother and to the end of life will be free from danger.

He who closes his mouth and shuts his sense gates will be free from trouble to the end of life. He who opens his mouth and meddles with affairs cannot be free from trouble even to the end of life.

To recognize one's insignificance is called enlightenment. To keep one's sympathy is called strength. He who uses Tao's light returns to Tao's enlightenment and does not surrender his person to perdition. This is called practicing the eternal.

LIII

GAIN BY INSIGHT

Even if one has but a little knowledge he can walk in the ways of the great Tao; it is only self-assertion that one need fear.

The great Tao (Way) is very plain, but people prefer the bypaths. When the palace is very splendid, the fields are likely to be very weedy, and the granaries empty. To wear ornaments and gay colors, to carry sharp swords, to be excessive in eating and drinking, and to have wealth and treasure in abundance is to know the pride of robbers. This is contrary to Tao.

LIV

TO CULTIVATE INTUITION

The thing that is well planted is not easily uprooted. The thing that is well guarded is not easily taken away. If one has sons and grandsons, the offering of ancestral worship will not soon cease.

He who practices Tao in his person shows that his teh is real. The family that practices it shows that their teh is abounding. The township that practices it shows that their teh is enduring. The state that practices it shows that their teh is prolific. The empire that practices it reveals that teh is universal. Thereby one person becomes a test of other persons, one family of other families, one town of other towns, one county of other counties, and one empire of all empires.

How do I know that this test is universal? By this same Tao.

LV

TO VERIFY THE MYSTERIOUS

The essence of teh is comparable to the state of a young boy. Poisonous insects will not sting him, wild beasts will not seize him, birds of prey will not attack him. The bones are weak, the muscles are tender, it is true, but his grasp is firm.

He does not yet know the relation of the sexes, but he has perfect organs, nevertheless. His spirit is virile, indeed! He can sob and cry all day without becoming hoarse, his harmony (as a child) is perfect indeed!

To recognize this harmony (for growth) is to know the eternal. To recognize the eternal is to know enlightenment. To increase life (to cause things to grow) is to know blessedness. To be conscious of an inner fecundity is strength. Things fully grown are about to decay, they are the opposite of Tao. The opposite of Tao soon ceases.

LVI

THE TEH OF THE MYSTERIOUS

The one who knows does not speak; the one who speaks does not know. The wise man shuts his mouth and closes his gates. He softens his sharpness, unravels his tangles, dims his brilliancy, and reckons himself with the mysterious.

He is inaccessible to favor or hate; he cannot be reached by profit or injury; he cannot be honored or humiliated. Thereby he is honored by all.

LVII

THE HABIT OF SIMPLICITY

The empire is administered with righteousness; the army is directed by craft; the people are captivated by non-diplomacy. How do I know it is so? By this same Tao.

Among people the more restrictions and prohibitions there are, the poorer they become. The more people have weapons, the more the state is in confusion. The more people are artful and cunning the more abnormal things occur. The more laws and orders are issued the more thieves and robbers abound.

Therefore the wise man says: If a ruler practices wu wei the people will reform of themselves. If I love quietude the people will of themselves become righteous. If I avoid profit-making the people will of themselves become prosperous. If I limit my desires the people will of themselves become simple.

LVIII

ADAPTATION TO CHANGE

When an administration is unostentatious the people are simple. When an administration is inquisitive, the people are needy. Misery, alas, supports happiness. Happiness, alas, conceals misery. Who knows its limits? It never ceases. The normal becomes the abnormal. The good in turn becomes unlucky. The people's confusion is felt daily for a long time.

Therefore the wise man is square, yet does not injure, he is angular but does not annoy. He is upright but is not cross. He is bright but not glaring.

LIX

TO KEEP TAO

In governing the people and in worshipping heaven nothing surpasses moderation. To value moderation, one must form the habit early. Its early acquisition will result in storing and accumulating vitality. By storing and accumulating vitality nothing is impossible. •

If nothing is impossible then one is ignorant of his limits. If one does not know his limitations, one may possess the state. He who possesses moderation is thereby lasting and enduring. It is like having deep roots and a strong stem. This is of long life and enduring insight the Tao (way).

LX

TO MAINTAIN POSITION

One should govern a great state as one fries small fish (i.e., do not scale or clean them).

With Tao one may successfully rule the Empire. Ghosts will not frighten, gods will not harm, neither will wise men mislead the people. Since nothing frightens or harms the people, teh will abide.

LXI

THE TEH OF HUMILITY

A great state that is useful is like a bond of unity within the Empire; it is the Empire's wife.

The female controls the male by her quietude and submission. Thus a great state by its service to smaller states wins their allegiance. A small state by submission to a great state wins an influence over them. Thus some stoop to conquer, and others stoop and conquer.

Great states can have no higher purpose than to federate states and feed the people. Small states can have no higher purpose than to enter a federation and serve the people. Both alike, each in his own way, gain their end, but to do so, the greater must practice humility.

LXII

THE PRACTICE OF TAO

The Tao is the asylum of all things; the good man's treasure, the bad man's last resort. With beautiful words one may sell goods but in winning people one can accomplish more by kindness. Why should a man be thrown away for his evil? To conserve him was the Emperor appointed and the three ministers.

Better than being in the presence of the Emperor and riding with four horses, is sitting and explaining this Tao.

The reason the Ancients esteemed Tao was because if sought it was obtained, and because by it he that hath sin could be saved. Is it not so? Therefore the world honors Tao.

LXIII

A CONSIDERATION OF BEGINNINGS

One should avoid assertion (wu wei) and practice inaction. One should learn to find taste in the tasteless, to enlarge the small things, and multiply the few. He should respond to hatred with kindness. He should resolve a difficulty while it is easy, and manage a great thing while it is small. Surely all the world's difficulties arose from slight causes, and all the world's great affairs had small beginnings.

Therefore the wise man avoids to the end participation in great affairs and by so doing establishes his greatness.

Rash promises are lacking in faith and many things that appear easy are full of difficulties. Therefore the wise man considers every thing difficult and so to the end he has no difficulties.

LXIV

CONSIDER THE INSIGNIFICANT

That which is at rest is easily restrained, that which has not yet appeared is easily prevented.

The weak is easily broken, the scanty is easily
scattered. Consider a difficulty before it arises,
and administer affairs before they become dis-
organized. A tree that it takes both arms to
encircle grew from a tiny rootlet. A pagoda of
nine stories was erected by placing small bricks.
A journey of three thousand miles begins with
one step. If one tries to improve a thing, he mars
it; if he seizes it, he loses it. The wise man,
therefore, not attempting to form things does not
mar them, and not grasping after things he does
not lose them. The people in their rush for
business are ever approaching success but continually failing. One must be as careful to the
end as at the beginning if he is to succeed.

Therefore the wise man desires to be free from
desire, he does not value the things that are
difficult of attainment. He learns to be unlearned,
he returns to that which all others ignore. In that
spirit he helps all things toward their natural de-
velopment, but dares not interfere.

LXV

THE TEH OF SIMPLICITY

In the olden days those who obeyed the spirit
of Tao did not enlighten the people but kept them
simple hearted.

The reason people are difficult to govern is
because of their smartness; likewise to govern
a people with guile is a curse; and to govern
them with simplicity is a blessing. He who

remembers these two things is a model ruler. Always to follow this standard and rule is teh, the profound.

Profound teh is deep indeed and far reaching. The very opposite of common things, but by it one obtains obedient subjects.

LXVI

TO SUBORDINATE SELF

The reason rivers and seas are called the kings of the valley is because they keep below them.

Therefore the wise man desiring to be above his people must in his demeanor keep below them; wishing to benefit his people, he must ever keep himself out of sight.

The wise man dwells above, yet the people do not feel the burden; he is the leader and the people suffer no harm. Therefore the world rejoices to exalt him and never wearies of him.

Because he will not quarrel with anyone, no one can quarrel with him.

LXVII

THREE TREASURES

All the world calls Tao great, yet it is by nature immaterial. It is because a thing is seemingly unreal that it is great. If a man affects to be great, how long can he conceal his mediocrity?

Tao has three treasures which he guards and cherishes. The first is called compassion; the second is called economy; the third is called humility. A man that is compassionate can be truly brave; if a man is economical he can be generous; if he is humble he can become a useful servant.

If one discards compassion and is still brave, abandons economy and is still generous, forsakes humility and still seeks to be serviceable, his days are numbered. On the contrary if one is truly compassionate, in battle he will be a conqueror and in defence he will be secure. When even Heaven helps people it is because of compassion that she does so.

LXVIII

COMPLIANCE WITH HEAVEN

He who excels as a soldier is the one who is not warlike; he who fights the best fight is not wrathful; he who best conquers an enemy is not quarrelsome; he who best employs people is obedient himself.

This is the virtue of not-quarreling, this is the secret of bringing out other men's ability, this is complying with Heaven. Since of old it is considered the greatest virtue (teh).

LXIX

THE FUNCTION OF THE MYSTERIOUS

A military expert has said: I do not dare put myself forward as a host, but always act as a guest. I hesitate to advance an inch, but am willing to withdraw a foot.

This is advancing by not advancing, it is winning without arms, it is charging without hostility, it is seizing without weapons. There is no mistake greater than making light of an enemy. By making light of an enemy we lose our treasure.

Therefore when well-matched armies come to conflict, the one who is conscious of his weakness conquers.

LXX

THE DIFFICULTY OF UNDERSTANDING

My words are very easy to understand and very easy to put into practice, yet in all the world no one appears to understand them or to practice them.

Words have an ancestor (a preceding idea), deeds have a master (a preceding purpose), and just as these are often not understood, so I am not understood.

They who understand me are very few, and on that account I am worthy of honor. The wise man wears wool (rather than silk) and keeps his gems out of sight.

LXXI

THE DISEASE OF KNOWLEDGE

To recognize one's ignorance of unknowable things is mental health, and to be ignorant of knowable things is sickness. Only by grieving over ignorance of knowable things are we in

mental health. The wise man is wise because he
understands his ignorance and is grieved over
it.

LXXII

TO CHERISH ONE'S SELF

When people are too ignorant to fear the fear-
some thing, then it will surely come. Do not
make the place where they dwell confining, the
life they live wearisome. If they are let alone,
they will not become restless. Therefore the
wise man while not understanding himself regards
himself, while cherishing he does not overvalue
himself. Therefore he discards flattery and pre-
fers regard.

LXXIII

ACTION IS DANGEROUS

Courage carried to daring leads to death.
Courage restrained by caution leads to life.
These two things, courage and caution, are sometimes beneficial and sometimes harmful. Some
things are rejected by heaven, who can tell the
reason? Therefore the wise man deems all
acting difficult.

The Tao of heaven does not quarrel, yet it conquers. It speaks not, yet its response is good.
It issues no summons but things come to it
naturally because its devices are good. Heaven's
net is vast, indeed! its meshes are wide but it
loses nothing.

LXXIV
OVERCOMING DELUSIONS

If the people do not fear death, how can one frighten them with death? If we teach people to fear death, then when one rebels he can be seized and executed; after that who will dare to rebel?

There is always an officer to execute a murderer, but if one takes the place of the executioner, it is like taking the place of a skilled carpenter at his hewing. If one takes the place of the skilled carpenter he is liable to cut himself. (Therefore do not interfere with Tao.)

LXXV
LOSS BY GREEDINESS

Starvation of a people comes when an official appropriates to himself too much of the taxes. The reason a people are difficult to govern is because the officials are too meddlesome; the people make light of death because they are so absorbed in life's interests. The one who is not absorbed in life is more moral than he who esteems life.

LXXVI
BEWARE OF STRENGTH

When a man is living he is tender and fragile. When he dies he is hard and stiff. It is the same with everything, the grass and trees, in life, are tender and delicate, but when they die they become rigid and dry.

Therefore those who are hard and stiff belong to death's domain, while the tender and weak belong to the realm of life.

Therefore soldiers are most invincible when they will not conquer. When a tree is grown to its greatest strength it is doomed. The strong and the great stay below; the tender and weak rise above.

LXXVII

TAO OF HEAVEN

Tao of heaven resembles the stretching of a bow. The mighty it humbles, the lowly it exalts. They who have abundance it diminishes and gives to them who have need.

That is Tao of heaven; it depletes those who abound, and completes those who lack.

The human way is not so. Men take from those who lack to give to those who already abound. Where is the man who by his abundance can best serve the world?

The wise man makes but claims not, he accomplishes merit, yet is not attached to it, neither does he display his excellence. Is it not so?

LXXVIII

TRUST AND FAITH

In the world nothing is more fragile than water, and yet of all the agencies that attack hard substances nothing can surpass it.

Of all things there is nothing that can take the

place of Tao. By it the weak are conquerors of
the strong, the pliable are conquerors of the
rigid. In the world every one knows this, but
none practice it.

Therefore the wise man declares: he who is
guilty of the country's sin may be the priest at
the altar. He who is to blame for the country's
misfortunes, is often the Empire's Sovereign.
True words are often paradoxical.

LXXIX

ENFORCING CONTRACTS

When reconciling great hatred there will some
remain. How can it be made good?

Therefore the wise man accepts the debit side
of the account and does not have to enforce pay-
ment from others. They who have virtue (teh)
keep their obligations, they who have no virtue
insist on their rights. Tao of heaven has no favor-
ites but always helps the good man.

LXXX

CONTENTMENT

In a small country with few people let there
be officers over tens and hundreds but not to
exercise power. Let the people be not afraid of
death, nor desire to move to a distance. Then
though there be ships and carriages, they will
have no occasion to use them. Though there
be armor and weapons there will be no occasion
for donning them. The people can return to

knotted cords for their records, they can delight in their food, be proud of their clothes, be content with their dwellings, rejoice in their customs.

Other states may be close neighbors, their cocks and dogs may be mutually heard, people will come to old age and die but will have no desire to go or come.

LXXXI
THE NATURE OF THE ESSENTIAL

Faithful words are often not pleasant; pleasant words are often not faithful. Good men do not dispute; the ones who dispute are not good. The learned men are often not the wise men, nor the wise men, the learned. The wise man does not hoard, but ever working for others, he will the more exceedingly acquire. Having given to others freely, he himself will have in plenty. Tao of heaven benefits but does not injure. The wise man's Tao leads him to act but not to quarrel.

VALEDICTORY
PART OF THE 20TH SONNET

Common people are joyful; they celebrate a feast day; they flock to a pavilion in spring time. I alone am calm, as one who has as yet received no omen; I am as a babe who has not learned to smile. I am forlorn, like a homeless wanderer! Common people have plenty; I alone am in want. I am a foolish man at heart! I am ignorant. Common people are vivacious and smart, I alone am dull and confused.

Knowledge of the Tao, how vast! I am like a sailor far beyond a place of anchorage, adrift on a boundless ocean. Common people are useful, I am awkward. I stand in contrast to them — but oh, the prize I seek is food from our Mother Tao!

WU WEI

HENRI BOREL

PREFACE

THE following study on Laotzu's "Wu-Wei" should by no means be regarded as a translation or even as a free rendering of the actual work of that philosopher   I have simply endeavoured to retain in my work the pure essence of his thought, and I have given a direct translation of his essential truths in isolated instances only, the rest being for the most part a self-thought-out elaboration of the few principles enunciated by him.

My conception of the terms "Tao" and "Wu-Wei" is entirely different from that of most sinologues (such as Stanislas Julien, Giles, and Legge), who have translated the work "Tao-Teh-King." But this is not the place to justify myself.   It may best be judged from the following work whether my conception be reasonable or incorrect.

Little is contained in Laotzu's short, extremely simple book, the words of which may be said to be condensed into their purely primary significance — (a significance at times quite at variance with that given in other works to the same words *) — but this little is gospel.   Laotzu's work is no treatise on philosophy, but contains, rather, merely those truths to which this (un-

* By Confucius, for instance.

written) philosophy had led him. In it we find
no form nor embodiment, nothing but the quintessence of this philosophy.

My work is permeated with this essence, but
it is no translation of Laotzu. None of my
metaphorical comparisons, such as that with the
landscape, with the sea, with the clouds, are anywhere to be found in Laotzu's work. Neither
has he anywhere spoken of Art, nor specially of
Love. In writing of all this I have spoken aloud
the thoughts and feelings instinctively induced
by the perusal of Laotzu's deep-felt philosophy.
Thus it may be that my work contains far more
of myself than I am conscious of; but even so,
it is but an outpouring of the thought and feeling
called up in me by the words of Laotzu.

I have made use of none but *Chinese* works on
Laotzu, and of those only a few. On reading
later some of the English and French translations,
I was amazed to find how confused and unintelli-
gible these books were.

I adhered to my simple idea of Laotzu's work,
and of my work I could alter nothing, for I felt
the truth of it within me as a simple and natural
faith.

HENRI BOREL.

CONTENTS

The numbers in the text refer to notes by the author, which will be found at the end of the book.

CHAPTER I

TAO

I WAS standing in the Temple of Shien Shan on an islet in the Chinese Sea, distant a few hours' journey from the harbour of Hā Tó.

On either side rose mountain ranges, their soft outlines interwoven behind the island to the westward. To the eastward shimmered the endless Ocean. High up, rock-supported, stood the Temple, in the shadow of broad Buddha-trees.

The island is but little visited, but sometimes fisher-folk, fleeing before the threatening typhoon, anchor there when they have no further hope of reaching the harbour. Why the Temple exists in this lonely spot, no one knows; but the lapse of centuries has established its holy right to stand there. Strangers arrive but seldom, and there are only a hundred poor inhabitants, or thereabouts, who live there simply because their ancestors did so before them. I had gone thither in the hope of finding some man of a serious bent of mind with whom to study. I had explored the temples and convents of the neighborhood for more than a year, in search of earnest-minded priests capable of telling me what I was unable to learn from the superficial books on Chinese religion; but I found nothing but ignorant,

stupid creatures everywhere — kneeling to idols
whose symbolical significance they did not understand, and reciting strange "Sutras" not one
word of which was intelligible to them.[1] And
I had been obliged to draw all my information from
badly translated works that had received even
worse treatment at the hands of learned Euro-
peans than at those of the literary Chinese whom
I had consulted. At last, however, I had heard
an old Chinaman speak of "the Sage of Shien
Shan" as of one well-versed in the secrets of
Heaven and Earth; and — without cherishing
any great expectations, it is true — I had crossed
the water to seek him out.

This Temple resembled many others that I
had seen. Grimy priests lounged on the steps
in dirty-grey garments, and stared at me with
senseless grins. The figures of "Kwan Yin" and
"Cakyamuni" and "Sam-Pao-Fu" had been
newly restored, and blazed with all imaginable
crude colours that completely marred their former
beauty. The floor was covered with dirt and
dust, and pieces of orange-peel and sugar-cane
were strewn about. A thick and heavy atmosphere oppressed my breast.

Addressing one of the priests, I said:

"I have come to visit the philosopher. Does
not an old hermit dwell here, called after 'Laotzu'?"

With a wondering face he answered me:

"Laotzu lives in the top-most hut upon the
cliffs. But he does not like barbarians."

I asked him quietly:

"Will you take me to him, Bikshu, for a dollar?"

There was greed in his glance, but he shook his head, saying:

"I dare not; seek him yourself."

The other priests grinned, and offered me tea, in the hope of a tip. —

I left them, and climbed the rocks, reaching the top in half an hour; and there I found a little square stone hut. I knocked at the door, and, shortly after, heard some one draw back a bolt.

There stood the sage, looking at me.

And it was a revelation.

It seemed as though I saw a great light — a light not dazzling, but calming.

He stood before me tall and straight as a palm-tree. His countenance was peaceful as is a calm evening, in the hush of the trees, and the still moonlight; his whole person breathed the majesty of nature, as simply beautiful, as purely spontaneous, as a mountain or a cloud. His presence radiated an atmosphere holy as the prayerful soul in the soft after-gleam on a twilight landscape, — I felt uneasy under his deep gaze, and saw my poor life revealed in all its pettiness. I could not speak a word, but felt in silence his enlightening influence.

He raised his hand with a gesture like the movement of a swaying flower, and held it out to me — heartily — frankly. He spoke, and his voice was soft music, like the sound of the wind in the trees:

"Welcome, stranger! What do you seek of me? — old man that I am!"

"I come to seek a master," I answered humbly, "to find the path to human goodness. I have long searched this beautiful land, but the people seem as though they were dead, and I am as poor as ever."

"You err somewhat in this matter," said the sage. "Strive not so busily to be so very good. Do not seek it overmuch, or you will never find the true wisdom. Do you not know how it was that the Yellow Emperor [2] recovered his magic pearl? I will tell you.[3]

"The Yellow Emperor once travelled round the north of the Red Sea, and climbed to the summit of the Kuenlün mountains. On his return to the southward he lost his magic pearl. He besought his wits to find it, but in vain. He besought his sight to find it, but in vain. He besought his eloquence to find it, but that was also in vain. At last he besought Nothing, and Nothing recovered it. 'How extraordinary!' exclaimed the Yellow Emperor, 'that Nothing should be able to recover it!' Do you understand me, young man?"

"I think this pearl was his soul," I answered, "and that knowledge, sight and speech do but cloud the soul rather than enlighten it; and that it was only in the peace of perfect quietude that his soul's consciousness was restored to the Yellow Emperor. Is it so, Master?"

"Quite right; you have felt it as it is. And

do you know, too, by whom this beautiful legend
is told?"

"I am young and ignorant; I do not know."

"It is by Chuang-Tse, the disciple of Laotzu,
China's greatest philosopher.   It was neither
Confucius nor Mencius who spoke the purest wisdom in this country, but Laotzu.   He was the
greatest, and Chuang-Tse was his apostle.   You
foreigners cherish, I know, a certain well-meaning
admiration for Laotzu also, but I think but few
of you know that he was the purest human being
who ever breathed. — Have you read the 'Tao-
Teh-King'? and have you ever considered, I
wonder, what he meant by 'Tao'?"

"I should be grateful if you would tell me,
Master."

"I think I may well instruct you, young man.
It is many years since I have had a pupil, and I
see in your eyes no curiosity, but rather a pure
desire of wisdom, for the freeing of your soul.
Listen then.[4]

"Tao is really nothing but that which you
Westerns call 'God.'   Tao is the One; the beginning and the end.   It embraces all things,
and to it all things return.

"Laotzu wrote at the commencement of his
book the sign: Tao.   But what he actually meant
— the Highest, the One — can have no name, can
never be expressed in any sound, just because it is
The One.   Equally inadequate is your term 'God.'
— Wu — Nothing — that is Tao.   You do not
understand me? — Listen further!   There exists,

then, an absolute Reality — without beginning, without end — which we cannot comprehend, and which therefore must be to us as Nothing. That which we *are* able to comprehend, which has for us a relative reality, is in truth only appearance. It is an outgrowth, a result of absolute reality, seeing that everything emanates from, and returns to, that reality. But things which are real to us are not real in themselves. What we call Being is in fact Not-Being, and just what we call Not-Being is Being in its true sense. So that we are living in a great obscurity. What we imagine to be real is not real, and yet emanates from the real, for the Real is the Whole. Both Being and Not-Being are accordingly Tao. But above all never forget that 'Tao' is merely a sound uttered by a human being, and that *the idea is essentially inexpressible.* All things appreciable to the senses and all cravings of the heart are unreal. Tao is the source of Heaven and Earth. One begat Two, two begat Three, Three begat Millions. And Millions return again into One.

"If you remember this well, young man, you have passed the first gateway on the path of Wisdom.

"You know, then, that Tao is the source of everything; of the trees, the flowers, the birds; of the sea, the desert, and the rocks; of light and darkness; of heat and cold; of day and night; of summer and winter, and of your own life. Worlds and oceans evaporate in Eternity. Man rises out of the darkness, laughs in the glimmer-

ing light, and disappears. But in all these
changes the One is manifested. Tao is in everything. Your soul in her innermost is Tao. —
"You see the world outspread before you, young
man? . . ."

With a stately gesture he pointed seawards.

The hills on either side stood fast, uncompromising, clear-set in the atmosphere — like strong
thoughts, petrified, hewn out by conscious energy
— yielding only in the distance to the tender
influence of light and air. On a very high point
stood a lonely little tree, of delicate leafage, in a
high light. The evening began to fall, with tender
serenity; and a rosy glow, dreamy yet brilliant,
lent to the mountains, standing ever more sharply
defined against it, an air of peaceful joyousness.
In it all was to be felt a gentle upward striving, a
still poising, as in the rarefied atmosphere of conscious piety. And the sea crept up softly, with
a still-swaying slide — with the quiet, irresistible
approach of a type of infinity. The sail of a little
vessel, gleaming softly golden, glided nearer.
So tiny it looked on that immense ocean — so
fearless and lovely! All was pure — no trace
of foulness anywhere.

And I spoke with the rare impulse of a mighty
joy.

"I feel it now, O Master! That which I seek
is everywhere. I had no need to seek it in the
distance; for it is quite close to me. It is everywhere — what I seek, what I myself am, what
my soul is. It is familiar to me as my own self.

It is all revelation! God is everywhere! Tao is in everything!"

"That is so, boy, but confuse it not! In that which you see is Tao, but Tao is not what you see. You must not think that Tao is visible to your eyes. Tao will neither waken joy in your heart nor draw your tears. For all your experiences and emotions are relative and not real.

"However, I will speak no more of that at present. You stand as yet but at the first gate, and see but the first glint of dawn. It is already much that you should realize Tao as present in everything. It will render your life more natural and confident — for, believe me, you lie as safe in the arms of Tao as a child in the arms of its mother. And it will make you serious and thoughtful too, for you will feel yourself to be in all places as holy a thing as is a good priest in his temple. No longer will you be frightened by the changes in things, by life and death; for you know that death, as well as life, emanates from Tao. And it is so natural that Tao, which pervaded your life, should also after death continually surround you.

"Look at the landscape before you! The trees, the mountains, the sea, they are your brothers, like the air and the light. Observe how the sea is approaching us! So spontaneously, so naturally, so purely 'because so it must be.'— Do you see your dear sister the little tree on yonder point, bending towards you? and the simple movement of her little leaves? — Then I will speak to you of Wu-Wei,[5] of 'non-resistance,' of 'self-movement' on the breath of your impulse as it was born out of Tao. Men would be true men if they would but let their lives flow of themselves, as the sea heaves, as a flower blooms, in the simple beauty of Tao. In every man there is an impulse towards that movement which, proceeding from Tao, would urge him back to Tao again. But men grow blind through their own senses and lusts. They strive for pleasure, desire, hate, fame and riches. Their movements are fierce and stormy, their progress a series of wild uprisings and violent falls. They hold fast to all that is unreal. They desire too many things to allow of their desiring the One. They desire, too, to be wise and good, and that is worst of all. They desire to know too much.

"The one remedy is: the return to the source whence they came. In us is Tao. Tao is rest. Only by renunciation of desire — even the desire for goodness or wisdom — can we attain rest. Oh! all this craving to know what Tao is! And this painful struggle for words in which to express it and to inquire after it! — The truly wise follow the Teaching which is wordless — which remains unexpressed.[6] And who shall ever express it? Those who know it (what Tao is) tell it not; those who tell it know it not.[7] Even I shall not tell you what Tao is. Yourself must discover it in that you free yourself from all your passions and cravings, and live in utter spontaneity, void of unnatural striving. Gently must Tao be

approached, with a motion reposeful as the movement of that broad ocean. That moves, not
because it·chooses to move, nor because it knows
that it is wise or good to move; it moves involuntarily, unconscious of movement. Thus will you
also return to Tao, and when you are returned you
will know it not, for you yourself will be Tao."

He ceased speaking, and looked at me gently.
His eyes shone with a quiet light, still and even as
the tint of the heavens.

"Father," I said, "what you say is beautiful
as the sea, and it seems simple as nature; but
surely it is not so easy — this strifeless, inactive
absorption of man into Tao?"

"Do not confuse words one with another,"
he replied. "By strifelessness — Wu-Wei — Laotzu did not mean common inaction, — not mere
idling, with closed eyes. He meant: relaxation
from earthly activity; from desire — from the
craving for unreal things. But he *did* exact
activity in *real* things. He implied a powerful
movement of the soul, which must be freed from
its gloomy body like a bird from its cage. He
meant a yielding to the inner motive-force which
we derive from Tao and which leads us to Tao
again. And, believe me: this movement is as
natural as that of the cloud above us. . . ."

High in the blue ether over our heads were
golden clouds, sailing slowly towards the sea.
They gleamed with a wonderful purity, as of a
high and holy love. Softly, softly they were
floating away.

"In a little while they will be gone, vanished in
the infinity of the heavens," said the hermit,
"and you will see nothing but the eternal
blue. Thus will your soul be absorbed into
Tao."

"My life is full of sins," I answered; "I am
heavily burdened with darkening desires. And so
are my benighted fellow-men. How can *our* life
ever — thus ethereally, in its purest essence —
float towards Tao? It is so heavy with evil,
it must surely sink back into the mire."

"Do not believe it, do not believe it!" he exclaimed, smiling in gracious kindliness. "No
man can annihilate Tao, and there shines in each
one of us the inextinguishable light of the soul.
Do not believe that the evilness of humanity is
so great and so mighty. The eternal Tao dwells
in all; in murderers and harlots as well as in
philosophers and poets. All bear within them
an indestructible treasure, and not one is better
than another. You cannot love the one in
preference to the other; you cannot bless the one
and damn the other. They are as alike in essence
as two grains of sand on this rock. And not one
will be banished out of Tao eternally, for all
bear Tao within them. Their sins are illusive,
having the vagueness of vapours. Their deeds
are a false seeming; and their words pass away
like ephemeral dreams. They cannot be 'bad,'
they cannot be 'good' either. Irresistibly they
are drawn to Tao, as yonder waterdrop to the
great sea. It may last longer with some than

with others, that is all. And a few centuries —
what matter they in the face of Eternity? — Poor
friend! Has your sin made you so fearful?
Have you held your sin to be mightier than Tao?
Have you held the sin of men to be mightier than
Tao? — You have striven to be good overmuch,
and so have seen your own misdoing in a falsely
clear light. You have desired overmuch goodness in your fellow-men also, and therefore has
their sin unduly troubled you. But all this is
a seeming. Tao is neither good nor bad. For
Tao is real. Tao alone *is;* and the life of all
unreal things is a life of false contrasts and relations, which have no independent existence, and
do greatly mislead. So, above all, do not desire
to be good, neither call yourself bad. Wu-Wei —
unstriving, self-impelled — that must you be.
Not bad — not good; not little — and not great;
not low — and not high. And only then will
you in reality *be*, even whilst, in the ordinary sense
you are not. When once you are free from all
seeming, from all craving and lusting, then will
you move of your own impulse, without so much
as knowing that you move; and this, the only
true life-principle — this free, untrammelled motion towards Tao — will be light and unconscious as the dissolution of the little cloud above
you."

I experienced a sudden sense of freedom. The
feeling was not joy — not happiness. It was
rather a gentle sense of expansion — a widening
of my mental horizon.

"Father," I said, "I thank you! This revelation of Tao lends me already an impulse which, though I cannot explain it, yet seems to bear me gently forward.

"How wonderful is Tao! With all my wisdom — with all my knowledge, I have never felt this before!"

"Crave not thus for wisdom!" said the philosopher. "Do not desire to know too much — so only shall you grow to know intuitively; for the knowledge acquired by unnatural striving only leads away from Tao. Strive not to know all there is to know concerning the men and things around you, nor — and this more especially — concerning their relations and antagonisms. Above all, seek not happiness too greedily, and be not fearful of unhappiness. For neither of these is real. Joy is not real, nor pain either. Tao would not be Tao, were you able to picture it to yourself as pain, as joy, as happiness or unhappiness; for Tao is One Whole, and in it no discords may exist. Hear how simply it is expressed by Chuang-Tse: 'The greatest joy is no joy.' And pain too will have vanished for you! You must never believe pain to be a real thing, an essential element of existence. Your pain will one day vanish as the mists vanish from the mountains. For one day you will realize how natural, how spontaneous are all facts of existence; and all the great problems which have held for you mystery and darkness will become Wu-Wei, quite simple, non-resistent, no longer a source of marvel to you. For everything grows out of Tao, everything is a natural part of the great system developed from a single principle. — Then nothing will have power to trouble you nor to rejoice you more. You will laugh no more, neither will you weep. — I see you look up doubtfully, as though you found me too hard, too cold. Nevertheless, when you are somewhat further advanced you will realize that *this* it means, to be in perfect sympathy with Tao. Then, looking upon 'pain,' you will know that one day it must disappear, because it is unreal; and looking upon 'joy,' you will understand that it is but a primitive and shadowy joy, dependent upon time and circumstance, and deriving its apparent existence from contrast with pain. Looking upon a goodly man, you will find it wholly natural that he should be as he is, and will experience a foreshadowing of how much goodlier he will be in that day when he shall no longer represent the 'kind' and 'good.' And upon a murderer you will look with all calmness, with neither special love nor special hate; for he is your fellow in Tao, and all his sin is powerless to annihilate Tao within him. Then, for the first time, when you are Wu-Wei at last — not, in the common human sense, existing — then all will be well with you, and you will glide through your life as quietly and naturally as the great sea before us. Naught will ruffle your peace. Your sleep will be dreamless, and consciousness of self will bring no care.[8] You will see Tao in all

things, be one with all existence, and look round
on the whole of nature as on something with
which you are intimate as with yourself. And
passing with calm acceptance through the changes
of day and night, summer and winter, life and
death, you will one day enter into Tao, where
there is no more change, and whence you issued
once as pure as you now return."

"Father, what you say is clear — and compels
belief. But life is still so dear to me, and I am
afraid of death; I am afraid too lest my friends
should die, or my wife, or my child! Death seems
to me so black and gloomy — and life is bright —
bright — with the sun, and the green and flowery
earth!"

"That is because you fail as yet to feel the perfect naturalness of death, which is equal in reality
to that of life. You think too much of the insignificant body, and the deep grave in which
it must lie; but that is the feeling of a prisoner
about to be freed, who is troubled at the thought
of leaving the dark cell where he has lived so
long. You see death in contrast to life; and
both are unreal — both are a changing and a
seeming. Your soul does not glide out of a
familiar sea into an unfamiliar ocean. That
which is real in you, your soul, can never pass
away, and this fear is no part of her. You must
conquer this fear for ever; or, better still, it will
happen when you are older, and have lived
spontaneously, naturally, following the motions
of Tao, that you will of your own accord cease

to feel it. . . . Neither will you then mourn for
those who have gone home before you; with
whom you will one day be reunited — not knowing, yourself, that you are reunited to them,
because these contrasts will no longer be apparent to you. . . .

". . . It came to pass once upon a time that
Chuang-Tse's wife died, and the widower was
found by Hui-Tse sitting calmly upon the ground,
passing the time, as was his wont, in beating
upon a gong. When Hui-Tse rallied him upon the
seeming indifference of his conduct, Chuang-Tse
replied:

"'Thy way of regarding things is unnatural.
At first, it is true, I was troubled — I could not
be otherwise. But after some pondering I reflected that originally she was not of this life,
being not only not born, but without form alto-
gether; and that into this formlessness no life-
germ had as yet penetrated. That nevertheless,
as in a sun-warmed furrow, life-energy then began
to stir; out of life-energy grew form, and form
became birth. To-day another change has com-
pleted itself, and she has died. This resembles
the rise and fall of the four seasons: spring,
autumn, winter, summer. She sleeps calmly in
the Great House. Were I now to weep and wail,
it were to act as though the soul of all this had not
entered into me, — therefore I do it no more.'" •

This he told in a simple, unaffected manner
that showed how natural it appeared to him.
But it was not yet clear to me, and I said:

"I find this wisdom terrible; it almost makes me afraid. Life would seem to me so cold and empty, were I as wise as this."

"Life *is* cold and empty," he answered, quietly, but with no trace of contempt in his tone; — "and men are as deceptive as life itself. There is not one who knows himself, not one who knows his fellows; and yet they are all alike. There is, in fact, no such thing as life; it is unreal."

I could say no more, and stared before me into the twilight. The mountains were sleeping peacefully in the tender, bloom-like shimmer of vague night-mists — lying lowly, like children, beneath the broad heavens. Below us was an indistinct twinkling of little red lights. From the distance rose a sad monotonous song, the wail of a flute accompanying it. In the depths of the darkness lay the sea in its majesty, and the sound of infinitude swelled far and wide.

Then there arose in me a great sadness, and my eyes filled, as with passionate insistence I asked him: "And what of friendship, then? — and what of love?" —

He looked at me. I could not see him plainly in the darkness, but there shone from his eyes a curious soft light, and he answered gently:

"These are the best things in life, by very far. They are one with the first stirring of Tao within you. But one day you will know of them as little as the stream knows of its banks when it is lost in the endless ocean. Think not that I would teach you to banish love from your heart;

for that would be to go against Tao. Love
what you love, and be not misled by the thought
that love is a hindrance which holds you in
bondage. To banish love from your heart would
be a mad and earthly action, and would put you
further away from Tao than you have ever been.
I say only, that love will one day vanish of itself
without your knowing, and that Tao is not
Love. But forget not, that — so far as I desire
it, and so far as it is good for you — I am speaking to you of the very highest things. Were
I only speaking of this life and of men, I should
say: Love is the highest of all. But for him
who is absorbed again into Tao, love is a thing
past and forgotten.

"Now, it has grown late, and I would not im-
part too much to you at first. You will surely
desire to sleep within the Temple, and I will
prepare your couch. Come with me — and de-
scend the mountain with all caution!"

He lit a little light, and held out his hand
to lead me. Slowly we proceeded, step by step.
He was as careful of me as though I had been his
child; he lighted my path at every steep descent,
and led me gently forward, taking heed of all my
movements.

When we arrived at the foot, he showed me the
little guest-chamber set apart for mandarins,[10]
and fetched pillow and covering for me.

"I thank you, Father, from my heart!" I said.
"When shall I ever be able to show my grati-
tude?"

He looked at me quietly, and the glance was great, like the sea. Calm he was, and gentle as night. He smiled at me, and it was like the light laughing upon the earth. And silently he left me.

CHAPTER II

ART

"WHAT is art?" I asked the hermit.

We were sitting upon the mountainside, in the shadow of an overhanging rock. Before us stretched the sea — one endless gleam of light in the sunshine. Golden sails were driving quietly over it, and white seagulls sweeping in noble curvings lightly hither and thither, while great, snow-pure clouds came up and sailed by in the blue, majestic in progress, steady and slow.

"It is as natural as the sea — the birds — the clouds," he answered. "I do not think you will find this so hard to grasp and feel as Tao. You have only to look around you — earth, clouds, atmosphere, everything will teach it you. Poetry has existed as long as heaven and earth.[11]

"Beauty was born with the heavens and the earth. The sun, the moon, and the red mists of morning and evening illumine each other, and yet — inexhaustible and wonderful as are the changes presented by them — Nature's great phenomena — there exist no pigments, as for garments, to dye them withal. All phenomena of the world bring forth sound when set in motion, and every sound implies some motion which has caused it. The greatest of all sounds are wind and thunder.

"Listen to the mountain stream racing over the rocks! As soon as it is set in motion the sound of it — high or low, short or long — makes itself heard, not actually according to the laws of music, it is true, yet having a certain rhythm and system.

"This is the spontaneous voice of heaven and earth; the voice that is caused by movement.

"Well! In the purest state of the human heart — when the fire of the spirit is at its brightest — then, if it be moved, that too will give forth sound. Is it not a wondrous metamorphosis that out of this a literature should be created?"

"So Poetry is the sound of the heart?"

"You will feel how natural this is. Poetry is to be heard and seen everywhere, for the whole of Nature is one great poet. But just because of its simplicity, therefore is it so strict and unalterable. Where the spring of movement is, there flows the sound of the poem. Any other sound is no poetry. The sound must come quite of itself — Wu-Wei — it cannot be generated by any artifices. There are many — how many! — who by unnatural movement force forth sound; but these are no poets — rather do they resemble apes and parrots. Few indeed are the true poets. From these the verse flows of itself, full of music, — powerful as the roaring of the torrent amongst the rocks, as the rolling of thunder in the clouds, — soft as the swishing of an evening shower, or the gentle breath of a summer night-breeze. — Hark!

hark to the sea at our feet! Is it not singing a
wondrous song? Is it not a very poem? — is
it not pure music? See how the waves sway, in
ceaseless mobility — one after the other — one
over the other — swinging onward and onward —
ever further and further — returning to vanish
in music once more! Dost thou hear their
rhythmic rushing? Oh! great and simple must
a poet be — like the sea! His movement, like
that of the sea, is an impulse out of Tao, and in
that — tranquil, strifeless, obedient as a child —
must he let himself go. Great, great is the sea!
Great, great is the poet. But greater — greater
— is Tao, that which is not great!"

He was silent, listening to the sea, and I saw
how the music of it entered into him.

I had reflected much since hearing his first words
concerning Tao. I was fearful lest his great and
lofty philosophy should mean death to the artist,
and that I also, in giving myself over to this
wisdom of his, should become incapable of feeling
the inspiration of the poet, and of being any more
childishly enraptured at the sight of beauty.

But he himself was standing there in the purest
ecstasy, as though he were now looking upon
the sea for the first time; and reverently, with
shining eyes, he listened to the rush of the waves.
"Is it not beautiful?" he said again, "is it not
beautiful, — this sound, that came out of Tao,
the soundless? — this light, that shone out of
Tao, the lightless? and the word-music: verse,
born of Tao the wordless? Do we not live in an

endless mystery? — resolving one day into absolute truth!"

I was a long time silent. But its very simplicity was hard for me to grasp. And I asked
him doubtfully: "Can it really be so easy — to
make and sing poems? It is surely not so easy
for us to bring forth verse as for the stream to
rush over the rocks? Must we not first practise
and train ourselves, and learn to know the verse-
forms thoroughly? And is not that voluntary
action, rather than involuntary motion?"

My question did not embarrass him, and he
answered at once: —

"Do not let that perplex you. All depends on
whether a man has in him the true spring from
which the verse should flow, or not. Has he
the pure impulse from Tao within him? or is his
life-motive something less simply beautiful? If
he *has* that source in him he is a poet, if he has it
not he is none. By this time you surely realize
that, considered from a high standpoint, all men
are really poets; for, as I have told you, there
exists in all men the essential, original impulse
emanating from and returning to Tao. But
rarely do we find this impulse alert and strongly
developed — rarely are men endowed with per-
ception of the higher revelations of beauty,
through which their bank-bound life-stream flows
till lost in boundless eternity. One might express
it thus: that ordinary men are like still water in
swampy ground, in the midst of poor vege-
tation; while poets are clear streams, flowing

amidst the splendour of luxuriant banks to the
endless ocean. But I would rather not speak
so much in symbols, for that is not plain enough.

"You would fain know whether a man who
has the true inspiration of the poet must not
nevertheless train himself somewhat in his art,
or whether he moves in it entirely of himself, like
nature? — The latter is without doubt the case!
For a young poet, having studied verse-form in
all its variety for but a short time, suddenly comes
to find these forms so natural as to preclude his
inclination for any other. His verse assumes
beautiful form involuntarily, simply because other
movement would be alien. That is just the difference between the poet and the dilettante:
that the poet sings his verse spontaneously, from
his own impulse, and afterwards, proving it, finds
it to be right in sound — in rhythm — in all its
movement; whereas the dilettante, after first
marking out for himself a certain verse-form,
according to the approved pattern of the art-
learned, proceeds to project by main force a series
of wholly soulless words upon it. The soulful
words of the poet flowed of themselves just because they were soulful. And, if we view things
in their true light, there do actually exist *no* hard
and fast forms for poetry, and absolutely no laws;
for a verse which flows spontaneously from its
source moves of itself, and is independent of all
preconceived human standards! The one law
is that there shall be no law. Mayhap you will
find this over-daring, young man! But remem-

ber that my demonstrations are taken not from men, but out of Tao, and that I know, moreover, but very few true poets. The man who is simple and pure as Nature is rare indeed. Think you that there are many such in your own land?"

This unexpected question embarrassed me, and I wondered what could be his drift. It was hard to answer, too, so I asked him first another question:

"Great Master, I cannot answer until I hear more from you. *Why does* a poet make a poem?"

That seemed to astonish him mightily, for he repeated it, as though doubting if he had heard aright:

"Why does a poet make a poem?"

"Yes, Master, why?"

Then he laughed outright, and said:

"Why does the sea roar? Why does the bird sing? Do you know that, my son?"

"Because they cannot help it, Father, because they simply must give their nature vent in that way! It is Wu-Wei!"

"Quite so! Well, — and why should it be different with a poet?"

I considered, and my answer came none too readily:

"Yes, but it *may* be different. A poet may sing for the sake of creating or enriching a literature, where there is none, or it is in danger of dying out. That has a fine sound, but is no pure motive. Or some poets sing in order to cover themselves with glory — to be famous, to be crowned with shining laurels, and to gain smiles from the fair, bright-eyed maidens strewing flowers on the path before them!"

"You must express yourself with greater exactness," said the hermit, "and not desecrate words which thousands hold sacred. For poets who sing for such reasons are no poets at all. A poet sings because he sings. He cannot sing with any given purpose, or he becomes a dilettante."

"Then, Father, supposing a poet to have sung as simply as a bird, may he afterwards take pleasure in the laurels and the roses? May he jealously hate those who wear the laurels of which he deems himself worthy? or can he believe his soul's convictions, and call beauty ugly, despising the beauty which he has created? — Can he call the beautiful hateful, because the laurels come from unwelcome hands? — Can he drape himself in a false garb, and elect to act differently from other men, in order to gain prominence through eccentricity? — Can he deem himself better than the common run of men? —Should he press the common hands which applaud him? — May he hate them who deride instead of honouring him? — How can you interpret to me all these things? They all appear so strange to me, in comparison with the little bird and the great sea!"

"All these questions, young friend, are an answer to *my* question," he replied; "for the fact that you would know all this is a proof that there are not many poets in your country. Re-

member that I understand and use the word
'poet' in its purest, highest meaning. A poet can
only live for his art, which he loves for itself, and
not as a means for securing fleeting earthly
pleasures. A poet looks upon men and things
— in their nature and relationship — so simply,
that he himself approaches very nearly to the
nature of Tao. Other men see men and things
hazily, as through a fog. The poet realizes this
to be an incontestable fact. How then can he
expect his simplicity to be understood — by this
hazy mind of the public? How can he cherish
feelings of hate and grief when it ridicules him?
How feel pleasure when it should do him honour?
It is the same in this case as with the four 'seasons' of Chuang-Tse. There is nothing specially
agitating in it all, because it is the natural course
of things. Consequently the poet is neither in
despair when he is not heard, nor happy when
he is fêted. He looks upon the state of things
with regard to the multitude and the way it com-
ports itself towards him as a natural consequence,
of which he knows the cause. The judgment of
the common people is not even so much as in-
different to him — it simply does not exist for
him. He does not sing his verses for the sake
of the people, but because he cannot help himself.
The sound of human comment on his work escapes
him entirely, and he knows not whether he be
famous or forgotten. 'The highest fame is no
fame.' * You look at me, young man, as

* From the "Nan Hwa King," chap. xviii.

though I were telling stranger things than you
have ever dared to dream. But I am telling
nothing but the plainest truth, simple and natural
as the truth in landscape or sea. Having dwelt
until so lately mid the strenuous life of your coun-
trymen, you have never yet seen true simplicity.
For so long you have heard nothing spoken of
but 'fame,' 'earnings,' 'honour,' 'artists' and
'immortality,' that, for all you know, these things
may be indispensable as air, and veritable as
your soul. But it is all a seeming and deception.
Those whom you have seen may indeed have
been poets of true fibre, but they had been led
astray from the impulse derived from Tao which
was their life-principle, and they did not remain
what they were, but sank through their weakness
to the nature of commonplace men. So that
they have come to do as ordinary men do, only
they do it more strongly. So much do I gather
from your questioning. But all these are poets no
longer, and will sing no more true poetry so long
as they remain as they are. For the smallest
deviation from the original impulse is sufficient
to kill the poetry within them. There is but
the one direct way: single and simple as a maid-
en — uncompromising as a straight line. This
straight line is spontaneity; on either side of it lie
false activity and the unnatural — also the roads
to fame and notoriety, where occur murder, and
sudden death, and where one bosom friend will
suck the life-blood from another to further the
attainment of his own ends. The straight line

cuts its own way, without deviation or secret
windings, in simple continuance into infinity.

"You understand then, that thus, by the
nature of things, all those situations which would
convert the poet into the sacrificial victim of the
mob become impossible. You have probably
read, in the history alike of your country and
my own, of poets who have died of grief at want
of recognition, or who have taken their own lives
on account of undeserved contumely. I have
indeed always felt the pathos of this, yet have
realized that to such poets as these the term
truly great cannot be applied.

"And I am speaking, of course, not of the artists of speech only, but of all artists. Shall I
show you now something by an artist as true and
simple-minded as I can conceive a man to be? —
Come with me then!"

He led me into a small chamber in his hut —
a cell with white walls and no furniture save
the bed, a table covered with books, and a few
chairs. He opened a door in the wall, and drew
out from it a wooden chest. This he carried
as carefully as though it had been some sacred
object or a little child. He set it gently down
upon the floor, opened the lid, and lifted out a
closed shrine of red-brown wood, which he placed
upon the table.[12]

"See," he remarked, "this is a beautiful shrine,
to begin with. A beautiful thing must have a
beautiful setting. At present the little doors are
shut. Do you not find this a goodly idea: to

be able ever thus to hold it hidden from profane
eyes? — But before *you* I may well open it."

And the two wings of the shrine flew apart.

Against a background of pale blue silk appeared a large figure, gleaming, and shimmer-
.ing, and diffusing a wonderful radiance of its own.
It was the Buddha Kwan Yin, seated upon a lotus
that reared itself, straight, and graceful, and
modestly opened, above a tumult of wild waves.[12]

"Do you perceive the utter simplicity and
beauty of this?" he asked me; and in his voice
there spoke a great and tender love. "Is not
this the very embodiment of perfect rest? — How
serene is the countenance — how wonderfully
tender, and yet how tensely grave, with its closed
eyes gazing into infinity! — See — the cheek, —
how delicate and tender! See — the mouth —
and the lofty curving of the eyebrows — and the
pure pearl gleaming above her forehead [14] —
symbol of a soul taking its flight from the body!
And the body — how few are the lines of it! Yet
see: what infinite love and mercifulness in the
downward pose of the left arm; and in the uplifted
right arm — with two raised fingers, held together
as in the act of preaching — what an indescrib-
able holiness! And how beautiful the repose
of the crossed legs resting so softly upon the lotus!
— And see — how tenderly felt, notwithstanding
the immense strength and restraint of the whole —
the delicate soles of the feet, curved with such
subtle gentleness! — Is it not the quintessence
of the whole of Buddhism in a single picture?

You need not to have read anything of Buddhism
in order to appreciate it now, here, in all its inmost meaning. Rest — is it not absolute rest —
this ideally pure countenance gazing thus stilly
into eternity? Love — is it not absolute love
for the world — this simple drooping of the arm?
And is not the essence of the whole doctrine
grasped and confined in the pose of the uplifted
fingers?

"And then — the material of which such a figure
as this is made! So you realize, I wonder, that
an artist such as this must have laboured for
years and years before his material became as
pure and ethereal as he required it to be? For
the nature of stone is so hard — is it not? — and
the general idea of it: matter — that would suit
but ill for the plastic representation of the ideal
conception: Rest. — So the artist wrought upon
all kinds of common materials such as clay, sand,
and earth, and transformed them, by means of
fit and harmonious combination with precious
stones, pearls, and jasper, into costly substances.
And so the material for this figure became something that was no longer material, but rather the
incarnation of a sublime idea. The artist wished
to symbolize also in his representation the rosy
dawn which broke upon mankind on the appearance of Buddha; and so, shimmering through the
snowy white of his porcelain, he introduced just
such a vague rosy glow as plays upon the morning clouds before the glory of the sun bursts forth.
Is not this half-realized, growing light more in-

stinct with feeling than light itself? Can you perceive this most indefinite, yet clear and rosy colour shimmering throughout the white? Is it not chaste as the first soft blush of a maiden? Is it not the godly love of the artist which thus glows in the pureness of the white? Such a figure is, in fact, no longer a figure. The idea of material is entirely obliterated; it is an inspiration."

For a long time I was too much moved to speak. More strongly yet than the pure wisdom of the old man, did the beauty of this art take hold upon and purify my soul. At last I asked gently:

"Who has created this marvel? I would fain know, that I may hold his name with yours in veneration."

"That is of little importance, my young friend!" he answered. "The soul that was in this artist is absorbed again into Tao, just as yours will be one day. His body has fallen away, like the leaves from a tree, just as yours in time will fall away. What weight can attach then to his name? Nevertheless, I will tell it you; he was called Tan Wei,[15] and he engraved this name in finely-devised characters upon the back of the figure, such being the custom at that time. — Who was he? A common workman, surely, who did not even know, himself, that he was an artist; who seemed to himself nothing more than a common peasant, and who had not the least suspicion that his work was so beautiful. But he must have gazed much at the heavens and clouds above him, and have loved the wide seas, and the landscapes,

and the flowers; otherwise he could not have
been so fine in feeling; for such simple lines and
pure colours are only to be found in Nature. He
was certainly not celebrated; you will not find
his name in any history. I could not tell you
whence he came, how he lived, or to what age.
I know only that it is more than four hundred
years since such figures as these were made, and
that connoisseurs reckon that this one dates from
the first half of the Ming-Dynasty. Most probably the artist lived quite quietly the same sort
of life as the other people, worked industriously
as a common labourer, and died humbly, unconscious of his own greatness. But his work
remained, and this image, which by a fortunate
chance has found its way to this district, where
the last wars never raged, is still the same as
when he made it. And thus it may last on for
centuries and centuries, in inextinguishable radiance, in maidenly majesty. O, to create such
a thing, in pure, unconscious simplicity — that
is to be a poet! That is the art which dates not
from time but from eternity! — How beautiful
it is! Do you not find it so too? This porcelain,
that is almost indestructible; this radiance, which
never dies away! Here upon the earth it stands,
so strong and yet so tender, and so it will be, long
after our successors are dead! — And the soul
of the artist is with Tao!"

We continued long to look upon the image.
Then he took careful hold of the shrine once more.

"It is so delicate," he said, "that I hardly dare

to expose it to broad daylight. For this miracle of tenderness — ethereal as a soul — the daylight is too hard. I feel a kind of anxiety lest the light should suddenly break it in pieces; or cause it to dissolve like a little light cloud — so wholly soul-like is its composition!"

And softly, very softly, he replaced the shrine within the chest, which he closed.

He went out now, before me, and we seated ourselves again beneath the overhanging rock.

"How beautiful it would be," I said, "if every one could make things like that, in all simplicity, and surround themselves with them, everywhere!"

"Every one!" he answered; "well, that is perhaps too much to expect! But there really was once a time when this great kingdom was one great temple of art and beauty. You may still see the traces of it here in China. At that time the greater number of the people were simple-minded artists. All objects surrounding them were beautiful, the smallest thing as well as the greatest — whether it were a temple, a garden, a table, a chair, or a knife. Just examine the little tea-cups, or the smallest censers of that period! The poorest coolie ate out of vessels as perfect in their way as my Kwan-Yin image. All objects were beautifully made, and involuntarily so. The simple artisans did not consider themselves 'artists,' or in any way different from their fellow-men, and no petty strife can have arisen between them, otherwise there would have been an end of their art. Everything was

beautiful because they were all single-minded
and worked honestly. It was as natural in those
days for things to be beautiful as it is now-a-days
for them to be ugly. The art of China has sunk
to its lowest ebb; that is a consequence of its
miserable social condition. You have surely
remarked that the art of the country is deteriorat-
ing. And that is a death-sign for this great Empire. For Art is inseparably connected with the
full-bloom of a country's life. If the art declines,
then the whole country degenerates. I do not
mean this in the political, but rather in the moral
sense. For a morally-strong and simple-hearted
people brings forth involuntarily a strong and
healthy art. — Yes, what you said is true; how
much better would men's lives be, could they
but create for themselves better surroundings!
And how extraordinary that this is not done!
For Nature remains ever and everywhere ac-
cessible to them. See the clouds — the trees —
the sea!"

The sea was still, as ever, splashing at our
feet — boundless and pure. Clouds sailed ma-
jestically landwards, with a slow motion, in the
full blaze of the light. Golden gleams, falling
upon the mountains, vanished again with the
rhythmical sweep of the clouds. Light and
motion, sound and play of colour, everywhere!

The hermit gazed calmly and confidingly at
this infinite loveliness; as though deeply conscious
of the intimate relationship existing between him
and all his surroundings. He seemed to guess

what was in my mind as I looked at him, for he
said:

"We fit as naturally into this beauty around us
as a tree or a mountain. If we can but remain
so always, we shall retain the feeling of our own
well-being amid all the great workings of the
world-system. So much has been said about
human life; and scholars have created such an
endless labyrinth of theories! And yet in its inmost kernel it is as plain as Nature. All things
are equal in simplicity, and nothing is really in
confusion, however much it may seem as though
it were so. Everything moves surely and inevitably as the sea."

There rang in his voice both the great love of
the poet and the quiet assurance of the scholar
who takes his stand upon incontrovertible truth.

"Are you satisfied for to-day?" was his friendly
question; "and have I helped you forward a little?
Do you feel more clearly what poetry is?"

"Father," I answered, "your wisdom is poetry,
and your poetry is wisdom! How can that be?"

"That is quite true, from your point of view,"
he answered. "But you have yet to learn that
all these words are but a seeming. I know not
what my wisdom is, nor my poetry. It is all one.
It is so simple and natural when you understand
this! It is all Tao."

CHAPTER III

LOVE

ONCE more it was evening. We sat again upon the soft turf of the mountain-side, the quietness of our mood in sympathy with the solemn stillness of twilight. The distant mountain-ranges reposed in an atmosphere breathing reverence and devotion — they seemed to be kneeling beneath the heavens, beneath the slow-descending blessing of night. The isolated trees dotted here and there about the hills stood motionless, in a pause of silent worshipping. The rush of the sea sounded distant and indistinct, lost in its own greatness. Peace lay over everything, and soft sounds went up, as of prayer.

The hermit stood before me, dignified as a tree in the midst of Nature, and awe-inspiring as the evening itself.

I had returned to question him again. For my soul found no repose apart from him, and a mighty impulse was stirring within me. But now that I found myself near him, I hardly dared to speak; and indeed it seemed as though words were no longer necessary — as though everything lay, of itself, open and clear as daylight. How goodly and simple everything appeared that evening! Was it not my own inmost being that I recognized

in all the beauty around me? and was not the
whole on the point of being absorbed into the
Eternal?

Nevertheless I broke in upon this train of
feeling, and cleft the peaceful silence with my
voice:

"Father," I said sadly, "all your words have
sunk into my mind, and my soul is filled with the
balm of them. This soul of mine is no longer my
own — no longer what I used to be. It is as
though I were dead: and I know not what is
taking place within me — by day and by night —
causing it to grow so light, and clear, and vacant
in my mind. Father, I know it is Tao; it is
death, and glorious resurrection; but it is not
love; and without love, Tao appears to me but
a gloomy lie."

The old man looked round him at the evening
scene, and smiled gently.

"What *is* love?" he asked calmly. "Are you
sure about that, I wonder?"

"No, I am not sure," I answered. "I do not
know anything about it, but that is just the reason
of its great blessedness. Yes, do but let me express it! I mean: love of a maiden, love of a
woman.—I remember yet, Father, what it was
to me when I saw the maiden, and my soul knew
delight for the first time. It was like a sea, like
a broad heaven, like death. It was light — and
I had been blind! It hurt, Father — my heart
beat so violently — and my eyes burned. The
world was a fire, and all things were strange, and

began to live. It was a great flame flaring from out my soul. It was so fearful, but so lovely, and so infinitely great! Father, I think it was greater than Tao!"

"I know well what it was," said the sage. "It was Beauty, the earthly form of the formless Tao, calling up in you the rhythm of that movement by which you will enter into Tao. You might have experienced the same at sight of a tree, a cloud, a flower. But because you are human, living by desire, therefore to you it could only be revealed through another human being, a woman — because, also, that form is to you more easily understood, and more familiar. And since desire did not allow the full upgrowth of a pure contemplation, therefore was the rhythm within you wrought up to be wild tempest, like a storm-thrashed sea that knows not whither it is tending. The inmost essence of the whole emotion was not 'love,' but Tao."

But the calmness of the old sage made me impatient, and excited me to answer roughly:

"It is easy to talk thus theoretically, but seeing that you have never experienced it yourself, you can understand nothing of that of which you speak!"

He looked at me steadily, and laid his hand sympathetically on my shoulder.

"It would be cruel of you to speak thus to any one but me, young man! — I loved, before you drew breath in this world! At that time there lived a maiden, so wondrous to see, it was as if

she were the direct-born expression of Tao. For
me she was the world, and the world lay dead
around her. I saw nothing but her, and for me
there existed no such things as trees, men, or
clouds. She was more beautiful than this evening, gentler than the lines of those distant mountains, more tender than those hushed tree-tops;
and the light of her presence was more blessed to
see than the still shining of yonder star. I will
not tell you her story. It was more scorching
than a very hell-fire — but it was not real, and
it is over now, like a storm that has passed. It
seemed to me that I must die; I longed to flee from
my pain into death. — But there came a dawn-
ing in my soul, and all grew light and comprehensible. Nothing was lost. All was yet as it
had been. The beauty which I believed to have
been taken from me lived on still, spotless, in
myself. For not from this woman, — out of my
soul had this beauty sprung; and this I saw
shining yet, all over the world, with an everlasting
radiance, Nature was no other than what I had
fashioned to myself out of that shadowy form of
a woman. And my soul was one with Nature,
and floated with a like rhythm towards the eternal
Tao."

Calmed by his calmness, I said: "She whom
I loved is dead, Father — She who culled my soul
as a child culls a flower never became my wife.
But I have a wife now, a miracle of strength and
goodness, a wife who is essential to me as light
and air. I do not love her as I even now love the

dead. But I know that she is a purer human being than that other. How is it then that I do *not* love her so much? She has transformed my wild and troubled life into a tranquil march towards death. She is simple and true as Nature itself, and her face is dear to me as the sunlight."

"You love her, indeed!" said the sage, "but you know not what love means, nor loving. I will tell it you. Love is no other than the rhythm of Tao. I have told you: you are come out of Tao, and to Tao you will return. Whilst you are young — with your soul still enveloped in darkness — in the shock of the first impulse within you, you know not yet whither you are trending. You see the woman before you. You believe her to be that towards which the rhythm is driving you. But even when the woman is yours, and you have thrilled at the touch of her, you feel the rhythm yet within you, unappeased, and know that you must forward, ever further, if you would bring it to a standstill. Then it is that in the soul of the man and of the woman there arises a great sadness, and they look at one another, questioning whither they are now bound. Gently they clasp one another by the hand, and move on through life, swayed by the same impulse, towards the same goal. Call this love if you will. What is a name? I call it Tao. And the souls of those who love are like two white clouds floating softly side by side, that vanish, wafted by the same wind, into the infinite blue of the heavens."

"But that is not the love that I mean!" I cried. "Love is not the desire to see the loved one absorbed into Tao; love is the longing to be always with her; the deep yearning for the blending of the two souls in one; the hot desire to soar, in one breath with her, into felicity! And this always with the loved one alone — not with others, not with Nature. And, were I absorbed into Tao, all this happiness would be for ever lost! Oh let me stay here, in this goodly world, with my faithful companion! Here it is so bright and homely, and Tao is still so gloomy and inscrutable for me."

"The hot desire dies out," he answered calmly. "The body of your loved one will wither and pass away within the cold earth. The leaves of the trees fade in autumn, and the withered flowers droop sadly to the ground. How can you love that so much which does not last? However, you know, in truth, as yet, neither how you love nor what it is that you love. The beauty of woman is but a vague reflection of the formless beauty of Tao. The emotion it awakens, the longing to lose yourself in her beauty, that ecstasy of feeling which would lend wings for the flight of your soul with the beloved — beyond horizon-bounds, into regions of bliss — believe me, it is no other than the rhythm of Tao; only you know it not. You resemble still the river which knows as yet only its shimmering banks; which has no knowledge of the power that draws it forward; but which will one day inevitably flow out into the great ocean.

Why this striving after happiness, after human happiness, that lasts but a moment and then vanishes again? Chuang-Tse said truly: 'The highest happinesss is no happiness.' Is it not small and pitiable, this momentary uprising, and downfalling, and uprising again? This wavering, weakly intention and progress of men? Do not seek happiness in a woman. She is the joyful revelation of Tao directed towards you. She is the purest form in the whole of nature by which Tao is manifested. She is the gentle force that awakens the rhythm of Tao within you. But she is only a poor creature like yourself. And you are for her the same joyful revelation that she is to you. Fancy not that that which you perceive in her is that Tao, that very holiest, into which you would one day ascend! For then you would surely reject her when you realized what she was. If you will truly love a woman, then love her as being of the same poor nature as yourself, and do not seek happiness with her. Whether in your love you see this or not — her inmost being is Tao. A poet looks upon a woman, and, swayed by the 'rhythm,' he perceives the beauty of the beloved in all things — in the trees, the mountains, the horizon; for the beauty of a woman is the same as that of Nature. It is the form of Tao, the great and formless, and what your soul desires in the excitement of beholding — this strange, unspeakable feeling — is nothing but your oneness with this beauty, and with the source of this beauty — Tao. And the like is

experienced by your wife. Ye are for each
other angels, who lead one another to Tao un-
consciously."

I was silent for a while, reflecting. In the soft
colouring and stillness of the evening lay a great
sadness. About the horizon, where the sun had
set, there glimmered a streak of faint red light,
like dying pain.

"What is this sadness, then, in the Nature
around us?" I asked. "Is there not that in the
twilight as though the whole earth were weeping
with a grievous longing? See how she mourns,
with these fading hues, these drooping tree-tops,
and solemn mountains. Human eyes must fill
with tears, when this great grief of Nature looms
within their sight. It is as though she were
longing for her beloved — as though everything —
seas, mountains and heavens — were full of
mourning."

And the Sage replied: "It is the same pain
which cries in the hearts of men. Your own
longing quivers in Nature too. The 'Heimweh'
of the evening is also the 'Heimweh' of your soul.
Your soul has lost her love: Tao, with whom she
once was one; and your soul desires re-union
with her love. Absolute re-union with Tao — is
not that an immense love? — to be so absolutely
one with the beloved that you are wholly hers,
she wholly yours; — a union so full and eternal
that neither death nor life can ever cleave your
oneness again? So tranquil and pure that desire
can no more awaken in you — perfect blessedness

being attained, and a holy and permanent peace?
. . . For Tao is one single, eternal, pure infinitude of soul.

"Is that not more perfect than the love of a
woman? — this poor, sad love, each day of which
reveals to you some sullying of the clear life of the
soul by dark and sanguine passion? When you
are absorbed into Tao, then only will you be completely, eternally united with the soul of your
beloved, with the souls of all men, your brothers,
and with the soul of Nature. And the few moments of blessedness fleetingly enjoyed by all
lovers upon earth are as nothing in comparison
with that endless bliss: the blending of the souls
of all who love in an eternity of perfect purity."

A horizon of blessedness opened out before my
soul, wider than the vague horizon of the sea,
wider than the heavens.

"Father!" I cried in ecstasy, "can it be that
everything is so holy, and I have never known it?
— I have been so filled with longing, and so worn-
out with weeping; and my breast has been heavy
with sobs and dread. I have been so consumed
with fear! I have trembled at the thought of
death! I have despaired of all things being good,
when I saw so much suffering around me. I have
believed myself damned, by reason of the wild
passions, the bodily desires, burning within and
flaming without me — passions which, though
hating them, I still was, coward-like, condemned
to serve. With what breathless horror I have
realized how the tender, flower-like body of my

love must one day moulder and crumble away in the cold, dark earth! I have believed that I should never feel again that blessed peace at the look in her eyes, through which her soul was shining. And was it Tao! — was Tao really even then always within me, like a faithful guardian? and was it Tao that shone from her eyes? Was Tao in everything that surrounded me? in the clouds, the trees and the sea? Is the inmost being of earth and heaven, then, also the inmost being of my beloved and my own soul? Is it *that* for which there burns within me that mysterious longing which I did not understand, and which drove me so restlessly onward? I thought it was leading me away from the beloved and that I was ceasing to love her! — Was it really the rhythm of Tao, then, that moved my beloved too? — the same as that in which all nature breathes, and all suns and planets pursue their shining course throughout eternity? — Then all is indeed made holy! — then Tao is indeed in everything, as my soul is in Tao! Oh, Father, Father! it is growing so light in my heart! My soul seems to foresee that which will come one day; and the heavens above us, and the great sea, they foretell it too! See, how reverent is the pose of these trees around us — and see the lines of the mountains, how soft in their holy repose! All Nature is filled with sacred awe, and my soul too thrills with ecstasy, for she has looked upon her beloved!"

I sat there long, in silent, still forgetfulness. It was to me as though I were one with the soul

of my master and with Nature. I saw nothing
and heard nothing; — void of all desire, bereft of
all will, I lay sunk in the deepest peace. I was
awakened by a soft sound close by me. A fruit
had fallen from the tree to the ground behind us.
When I looked up, it was into shimmering moonlight. The recluse was standing by me, and bent
over me kindly.

"You have strained your spirit overmuch, my
young friend!" he said concernedly. "It is too
much for you in so short a time. You have fallen
asleep from exhaustion. The sea sleeps too.
See, not a furrow breaks its even surface; motionless, dreaming, it receives the benediction of
the light. But you must awaken! It is late,
your boat is ready, and your wife awaits you at
home in the town."

I answered, still half dreaming: "I would so
gladly stay here. Let me return, with my wife,
and stay here for ever! I cannot go back to the
people again! Ah, Father, I shudder — I can see
their scoffing faces, their insulting glances, their
disbelief, and their irreverence! How can I retain
the wondrous light and tender feeling of my soul
in the midst of that ungracious people? How can
I ever so hide it under smile or speech that they
shall never detect it, nor desecrate it with their
insolent ridicule?"

Then, laying his hand earnestly upon my
shoulder, he said:

"Listen carefully to what I now say to you, my
friend, and above all, *believe* me. I shall give you

pain, but I cannot help it. You *must* return to the world and your fellow-men; it cannot be otherwise. You have spoken too much with me already; perhaps I have said somewhat too much to you. Your further growth must be your own doing, and you must find out everything for yourself. Be only simple of heart, and you will discover everything without effort, like a child finding flowers. At this moment you feel deeply and purely what I have said to you. This present mood is one of the highest moments of your life. But you cannot yet be strong enough to maintain it. You will relapse, and spiritual feeling will turn again to words and theories. Only by slow degrees will you grow once more to feel it purely and keep it permanently. When that is so, then you may return hither in peace and then you will do well to remain here; — but by that time I shall be long dead.

"You must complete your growth in the midst of life, not outside it; for you are not yet pure enough to rise above it. A moment ago, it is true, you were equal even to that, but the reaction will soon set in. You may not shun the rest of mankind; they are your equals, even though they may not feel so purely as you do. You can go amongst them as their comrade, and take them by the hand; only do not let them look upon your soul, so long as they are still so far behind you. They would not mock you from evil-mindedness, but rather out of religious persuasion, being unaware how utterly miserable, how godless, how forsaken they are, and how far from all those holy things by which you actually live. You must be so strong in your conviction that nothing can hinder you. And that you will only become after a long and bitter struggle. But out of your tears will grow your strength, and through pain you will attain peace. Above all remember that Tao, Poetry and Love are one and the same, although you may seek to define it by these several vague terms; — that it is always within you and around you; — that it never forsakes you; and that you are safe and well cared for in this holy environment. You are surrounded with benefits, and sheltered by a love which is eternal. Everything is rendered holy through the primal force of Tao dwelling within it."

He spoke so gently and convincingly that I had no answer to give. Willingly I allowed myself to be guided by him to the shore. My boat lay motionless upon the smooth water, awaiting me. —

"Farewell, my young friend! Farewell!" he said, calmly and tenderly. "Remember all that I have told you!"

But I could not leave him in such a manner. Suddenly I thought of the loneliness of his life in this place, and tears of sympathy rose to my eyes. I grasped his hand.

"Father, come with me!" I besought him. "My wife and I will care for you; we will do everything for you; and when you are sick we will tend you. Do not stay here in this loneliness, so void of all the love that might make life sweet to you!"

He smiled gently, and shook his head as a father might at some fancy of his child's, answering with tranquil kindness:

"You have lapsed already! Do you realize now how necessary it is for you to remain in the midst of the every-day life? I have but this moment told you how great is the love which surrounds me — and still you deem me lonely here and forsaken? — Here, in Tao, I am as safe at home as a child is with its mother. You mean it well, my friend, but you must grow wiser, much wiser! Be not concerned for me; that is unnecessary, grateful though I am to you for this feeling. Think of yourself just now. And do what I say. Believe that I tell you that which is best for you. In the boat lies something which should remind you of the days you have spent here. Farewell!"

I bent silently over his hand and kissed it. I thought I felt that it trembled with emotion; but when I looked at him again his face was calm and cheerful as the moon in the sky.

I stepped into the boat, and the boatman took up the oars. With dextrous strokes he drove it over the even surface of the water. I was already some way from the land when my foot struck against some object in the boat and I remembered that something for me was lying there. I took it up. It was a small chest. Hastily I lifted the lid.

And in the soft, calm moonlight there gleamed with mystical radiance the wonderful porcelain of the Kwan-Yin image, the same which the old man had cherished so carefully, and loved so well.

There, in the lofty tranquility of severe yet gentle lines, in all the ethereal delicacy of the transparent porcelain, reposed the pure figure of Kwan-Yin, shining as with spiritual radiance amidst the shimmering petals of the lotus.

I scarcely dared believe that this holy thing had been given to me. I seized my handkerchief, and waved with it towards the shore, to convey to the recluse my thanks. He stood there motionless, gazing straight before him. I waited longingly for him to wave — for one more greeting from him — one more sign of love — but he remained immovable.

Was it I after whom he was gazing? Was he gazing at the sea? . . .

I closed the lid of the chest, and kept it near me, as though it had been a love of his which I was bearing away. I knew now that he cared for me; but his imperturbable serenity was too great for me — it saddened my mood that he had never signed to me again.

We drew further and further away; the outlines of his figure grew fainter and fainter; at last I could see it no more.

He remained; with the dreams of his soul, in the midst of Nature — alone in infinity — bereft of all human love — but close to the great bosom of Tao.

I took my way back to the life amongst mankind, my brothers and equals — in all the souls of whom dwells Tao, primordial and eternal.

The ornamental lights of the harbour gleamed already in the distance, and the drone of the great town sounded nearer and nearer to us over the sea.

Then I felt a great strength in me, and I ordered the boatman to row still more quickly. I was ready.   Was I not as safely and well cared for in the great town as in the still country? — in the street as on the sea?

In everything, everywhere, dwells Poetry — Love — Tao. And the whole world is a great sanctuary, well-devised and surely-maintained as a strong, well-ordered house.

NOTES

1. p. 62. This is a fact. Chinese priests are in the habit of repeating Sutras which, to judge by the sound, have been translated from the Sanscrit into Chinese phrases of which they do not understand one word.

2. p. 64. The "Yellow Emperor" is a legendary emperor, who appears to have reigned about the year 2697 B.C.

3. p. 64. That which follows in inverted commas is an extract translated from the twelfth chapter of the "Nan Hwa King."

4. p. 65. The following passage, as far as the sentence "and the Millions return again into One" is an adaptation — not a translation — of the first section of "Tao-Teh-King." Laotsu's wonderfully simple writing cannot possibly be translated into equally simple passages in our language. This rendering of mine — arrived at partly by aid of Chinese commentators — is an entirely · new reading, and is, to the best of my knowledge, the true one. One of the most celebrated, and, in a certain sense, one of the most competent of the sinologues, Herbert Giles, translates of this first section only the first sentence, and finds the rest not worth the trouble of translating! (compare "The Remains of Lao Tzü," by H. A. Giles, Honkong, *China Mail* Office, 1886). This same scholar translates "Tao" as "the Way," not perceiving how impossible it is that that which Laotsu meant — the highest of all, the infinite — should be a "way," seeing that a way (in the figurative sense) always leads to something else, and therefore cannot be the highest. Another still more celebrated sinologue, Dr.

Legge, translates "Tao" as "Course," and out of the simple
sentence: "If Tao could be expressed in words it would
not be the eternal Tao" he makes: "The Course that can
be trodden is not the enduring and unchanging course."
The whole secret is this: that the sign or word "Tao" has
a great number of meanings, and that in Confucius's work
"Chung Yung" it does as a matter of fact mean "Way";
but in a hundred other instances it means: "speech expression, a saying." Laotsu having, in one sentence, used this
sign in two different senses, nearly all translators have
suffered themselves to be misled. The sentence is as simple
as possible, and in two of my Chinese editions the commentators put: "spoken," and: "by word of mouth." But of
all the sinologues only Wells Williams has translated this
sentence well, namely thus: "The Tao which can be expressed is not the eternal Tao." Although the construction
of the phrase is not accurately rendered, at any rate Williams
has grasped the meaning.

After my work had already appeared in the periodical
De Gids, I saw for the first time Professor de Groot's work
"Jaarlijksche feesten en gebruiken der Emoy Chineesen,"
from which I gathered that he agreed with me in so far as
to say also that "Tao" was untranslatable — a sub-lying
conception "for which the Chinese philosopher himself
could find no name, and which he consequently stamped
with the word 'Tao.'" Professor de Groot adds: "If one
translates this word by 'the universal soul of Nature,' 'the
all-pervading energy of nature,' or merely by the word
'Nature' itself, one will surely not be far from the philosopher's
meaning."

Although the term holds for me something still higher
yet I find Professor de Groot's conception of it the most
sympathetic of all those known to me.

5. p. 69. This "Wu-Wei" — untranslatable as it is
in fact — has been rendered by these sinologues into "in-

action" — as though it signified idleness, inertia. It most
certainly does not signify idleness, however, but rather
action, activity — that is to say: "inactivity of the per-
verted, unnatural passions and desires," but "activity in
the sense of natural movement proceeding from Tao."
Thus, in the "Nan Hwa King" we find the following: "The
heavens and the earth do nothing" (in the evil sense) "and"
(yet) "there is nothing which they do not do." The whole
of nature consists in "Wu-Wei," in natural, · from-Tao-
emanating movement. By translating Wu-Wei into "inaction" the sinologues have arrived at the exact opposite
of the meaning of the Chinese text.   `

Laotsu himself does not dilate further upon the subject.
What follows here is my own conception of the text. The
whole first chapter of the original occupies only one page
in the book, and contains only fifty-nine characters. It
testifies to Laotsu's wonderful subtlety and terseness of
language that he was able in so few words to say so much.

6. p. 69. This sentence is translated from the "Tao-
Teh-King" (chapter ii).

7. p. 69. From the 56th chapter. This sentence is
also to be found in 15th chapter of the "Nan Hwa King."

8. p. 74. This runs somewhat as follows in the 6th
chapter of the Nan Hwa King: "The true men of the early
ages slept dreamlessly, and were conscious of self without care."

9. p. 76. This episode is translated from the 18th section of the "Nan Hwa King." By the "Great House"
Chuang-Tse meant, of course, the universe, and this expression "house" lends to the passage a touch of familiar
intimacy, showing Chuang-Tse to have the feeling that
the dead one was well cared for, as though within the shelter
of a house. — H. Giles, who renders it "Eternity," which
does not appear at all in the Chinese text, loses by his translation the confiding element which makes Chuang-Tse's
speech so touching. (Compare "Chuang Tsy," by H.

Giles, London, Bernard Quaritch, 1889.)   The actual words
are: "Ku Shih" = Great House.

10. p. 78. In almost all the temples is a chamber in
which the Mandarins lodge, and where Western travellers
may usually stay for the night, and probably for longer
periods.

11. p. 80. The following, to the end of the sentence:
"Poetry is the sound of the heart," has been translated
by me from a preface by Ong Giao Ki to his edition of the
Poetry of the Tang-Dynasty. Ong Giao Ki lived in the
first half of the eighteenth century.

12. p. 89. The Chinese do really preserve their treasures
in this careful manner. It is usual for an antique figure of
Buddha to lie in a silk-lined shrine, the shrine in a wooden
chest, and the chest in a cloth. It is unpacked upon great
occasions.

13. p. 90. Such a figure as the above-described is not
a mere figment of the author's imagination — such figures
really exist. A similar one is in the possession of the author.

14. p. 90. The Soul-Pearl "Durmâ."

15. p. 92. The figure in the author's possession is by
Tan Wei. Another great artist was Ho Chao Tsung, of
certain figures by whom I have also, with very great trouble,
become possessed. These names are well known to every
artist, but I have endeavoured in vain to discover anything
nearer with regard to them. They became famous after
death; but they had lived in such simplicity and oblivion,
that now not even their birthplace is remembered. One
hears conjectures, but I could arrive at no certainty.

Ingram Content Group UK Ltd.
Milton Keynes UK
UKHW021825240323
419083UK00005B/83